Prove All Things Workbook

by
R. S. "Bud" Miller, D.D.
Publisher
Betty Miller, D.M.
Author

Christ Unlimited — P.O. Box 850 — Dewey, AZ 86327   USA

Unless otherwise indicated, all Scripture quotations are taken from the <u>King James Version of the Holy Bible</u> (KJV).

<u>Overcoming Life Series:</u>

<u>Prove All Things Workbook</u>

ISBN 1-57149-001-9

Copyright © 1995-2013

R.S. "Bud" and Betty Miller

P. O. Box 850

Dewey, Arizona 86327

Published by

Christ Unlimited Publishing

P. O. Box 850

Dewey, Arizona 86327

www.BibleResources.org

Publisher: Pastor R. S. "Bud" Miller

Printed in the United States of America.

Contents

Christ Unlimited — P.O. Box 850 — Dewey, AZ 86327   USA

Personal Introduction

A lack of education will not hinder anyone from taking this course, and a doctor's degree will not help. However, one requirement that is necessary for this course to benefit the student is a <u>total commitment</u> to God. The Holy Spirit is our teacher, and we can learn if we come to God as little children. Being hungry to know God is a necessary prerequisite in order for this course to be of help.

If any of us are to receive truth, we must seek God, who is truth, with our whole hearts. We must seek Jesus first, then the knowledge of His Word will be revealed to us . Therefore, I want to emphasize once again the need to become as "a little child" in our approach to learning God's Word (Matthew 18:1-4; Jeremiah 29:13).

We need to come humbly before God, asking Him to remove any "know-it-all" attitudes, in order to be teachable. By laying down everything we thought we knew, we give God a chance to correct things we have believed that were wrong. Then we can begin to live the overcoming lives that God intended for His children to experience.

This course is part of a larger course based on the <u>Overcoming Life Series</u>, nine books taken from our first published book, <u>How To Overcome Through the Christ Unlimited</u>. That book, given to us under the anointing of the Holy Spirit, covers most of the basic things a Christian needs to know to get started on a victorious, overcoming walk with the Lord.

Christ Unlimited — P.O. Box 850 — Dewey, AZ 86327   USA

We have purposely kept this course simple for the average Christian who needs help in understanding how to study the Word and how to sort out principles and concepts when he, or she, reads the Bible; however, it also is for the seminary student. In addition, it is designed for students who desire to use it as a correspondence course. They can learn from it, even if they are totally alone and without a human teacher. The Holy Spirit always is there to teach us as we study about His Word.

On the other hand, groups with a teacher, or moderator, also can use this course to advantage. Our prayer is that however this course is taken, each student will complete it a different person and be conformed more into the image of Christ our Lord.

Bud and Betty Miller

Prove All Things Workbook

Section One

"Establishment in the Word"

Christ Unlimited — P.O. Box 850 — Dewey, AZ 86327   USA

Prove All Things Workbook
Section One: "Establishment in the Word"
Expository Introduction

[Author's Note: This workbook is the first in the Overcoming Life Series, which includes nine books and workbooks. Lessons also have supplementary material. Answers are provided at the end of the workbook and do not have to be the exact wording in many cases. The student simply needs to make sure that he, or she, has caught the concept or principle from the Word of God.]

Requirements for the Overcoming Life

Three things are necessary to live the overcoming life: a total commitment to Christ, a walk in the Spirit, and a good foundation in the Word of God. Let's consider these briefly one at a time:

1. A total commitment to Christ.

A half-hearted approach to God leaves a "door" open for deception. We must give God everything, because what we hold back for ourselves and do not place under the authority of the Holy Spirit will be enough to lead us astray at some point. That can cause our downfall in the Christian walk (Mark 12:30).

2. A walk in the Spirit

Galatians 5:25 says:

If we live in the Spirit, let us also walk in the Spirit.

Christ Unlimited — P.O. Box 850 — Dewey, AZ 86327   USA

If we are to live overcoming lives, we must daily walk in the guidance and direction of the Holy Spirit. From the above verse, we see that we can be Christians living in God's Spirit yet not necessarily "walking" in the Spirit. To be overcomers, we must walk in the Spirit by always choosing to do God's will in everything. That is what walking in the Spirit means.

3. A foundation in the Word.

To gain a foundation in the Word, we must give first place in our lives to the Word of God. If we have a problem, we should look first in the Bible for the answer and not to our own understanding and knowledge or to the world's knowledge. By putting the Word into practice in our lives, we will not be ashamed in any area (2 Timothy 2:15).

We should put the Word ahead of our desires, our feelings, and our thinking (Romans 12:1,2). We must walk by faith and not by sight (2 Corinthians 5:7). We should allow the Word of God to be the fin authority on every issue.

We should seek God's revelation knowledge in everything we approach as that kind of knowledge is given by the Holy Spirit to the heart of man. When seeking this revelation knowledge, we must have a standard by which to determine truth. That standard for Christians is the Bible, the inspired Word of God, which should be the source of all knowledge for us.

Man's knowledge, or worldly knowledge, is intellectual knowledge gained by mind study. The Bible says in Ecclesiastes 12:12 that this kind of study is a weariness of the flesh, and Ecclesiastes 1:18 says it brings grief and sorrow.

True revelation knowledge is taught by God to:

1. Those who have the proper foundation (Jesus, the cornerstone)

2. Those who are striving for maturity

3. Those who are filled with the Holy Spirit

Learning To Prove All Things

Since we already have seen that the Bible is the standard of truth for Christians, then obviously, the way to see if something is true is to see if it lines up with the Word of God. Each Christian has the responsibility to prove everything they hear by the Word and by the witness of the Holy Spirit to its truth.

Today, the world has no enduring standard. Every man does what is right in his own eyes, as Israel did in the day of the judges (Judges 17:6). A multitude of standards abound in the 20th century, ranging from the many cultic and false religious standards to our current cultural "standards."

Much of the confusion in the world today comes from this one thing: Society has abandoned the one standard of truth, which is the Bible. The Word of God is the final authority on all things, thus the world's standards all are doomed.

There is a way which seemeth right unto a man, but the end thereof are the ways of death.

Proverbs 14:12

Christ Unlimited — P.O. Box 850 — Dewey, AZ 86327   USA

Jesus said in **Matthew 7:24-27** that things built according to worldly standards will fall when storms come. Christians are not exempt from the storms of life. However, if our foundation is on Jesus, the Rock, then we will continue to stand and not be blown away when the storms come.

The Christian's standard has a two-fold nature: the written Word (the Bible) and the Living Word, Jesus Christ (**John 1:1-14**). As I emphasized earlier, we will not be able to discern truth from error nor to stand on the truth that is Jesus and live according to the truth that is the Bible — unless we are totally committed to God (**1 John 4:4-6**).

If we are committed to God, we will obey Him (**John 7:17, 14:21-24**). A true disciple and learner of Jesus is one who continues to obey the truth given to him (**John 8:31,32**). Disciple is the root word for discipline. Undisciplined lives reveal rebellion in them. Any rebellion should be repented of and given up in order to be a true disciple of Jesus.

Since Jesus returned to Heaven to sit at the right hand of the Father (**Acts 7:56; Colossians 3:1; Hebrews1:3**), the Holy Spirit is now our Teacher (**John 14:26**). In addition to speaking to us through the Word and directly to our hearts, the Holy Spirit speaks to us through our spiritual leaders. Also, He speaks to us through the books and lives of other Christians; however, He remains the Teacher.

God has supernaturally protected the Bible down through the centuries, and no other work on earth has been preserved in this way. Men have tried to destroy it, and wars have been fought over it, but it remains today.

The promises and principles of the Word have been proven to work in individual lives in every age and culture (**Hebrews 13:7,8**).

In studying the Word, we must keep our focus on the theme of the Bible — which is the redemption of man through the death of Christ on the cross and His resurrection. Those who make something other than this theme the focus of their lives, ministries, and teachings will fall into error.

This is how many cults have gotten started: by using parts of the Word out of context with the whole Bible. The purpose of the Bible is to bring the knowledge of God's redemption plan to mankind. The Holy Spirit inspired men to write of Jesus, in order that we might become like Him (**Romans 8:29**).

Lesson for Section One

[Author's Note: Material for this lesson is taken from the book <u>Prove All Things</u> and from the expository material in this workbook. All Scripture references that answer these questions have been given. Please do not look at the answers until the lesson is completed. This is an expository lesson to help you learn.]

I. Definition of Knowledge

Second Corinthians 4:1-7 tells us there are two kinds of knowledge. Define them according to the previous expository information and according to the Scriptures given.

A. Head Knowledge (2 Corinthians 4:4):

_____

_____

B. Heart Knowledge (2 Corinthians 4:6; Matthew 16:15-18).

_____

_____

. . . Much study is a weariness of the flesh.

Ecclesiastes 12:12

Also read Ecclesiastes 12:9-14.

For in much wisdom is much grief: and he that increaseth knowledge increaseth sorrow.

Ecclesiastes 1:18

The fear of the Lord is the beginning of knowledge: but fools despise wisdom and instruction.

Proverbs 1:7

And have put on the new man, which is renewed in knowledge after the image of him that created him.

Colossians 3:10

...Apply thine heart unto my knowledge.

Proverbs 22:17

Also read Proverbs 22:18-21.

II. Results of Lack of Knowledge

A. What is the consequence of lack of knowledge?

_____

My people are destroyed for lack of knowledge . . . .

Hosea 4:6

B. Is God talking about sinners or Christians in that verse?

_____

III. Knowledge and Obedience

A. Knowledge alone is not sufficient. What else is needed?
   Reference: Job 36:10-12

_____

But be ye doers of the word, and not hearers only, deceiving your own selves.

James 1:22

...Hear, O Israel, the statutes and judgments which I speak in your ears this day, that ye may learn them, and keep, and do them.

Deuteronomy 5:1

B. Obedience means being totally _____ to God.

IV. Learning Knowledge

   A. The Lord teaches knowledge to those who are:

     1. _____

     2. _____

     3. _____

Whom shall he teach knowledge? and whom shall he make to understand doctrine? them that are weaned from the milk, and drawn from the breasts. For precept must be upon precept, precept upon precept; line upon line, line upon line; here a little, and there a little: For with stammering lips and another tongue will he speak to this people.

Isaiah 28:9-11

Christ Unlimited — P.O. Box 850 — Dewey, AZ 86327   USA

Also read **Isaiah 28:16.**

    B. God teaches precept upon _____.

V. Submission and Knowledge

    A. Can zeal alone produce a victorious Christian walk?

    _____

    Reference: **Romans 10:2;** also read verses 1,3-5.

  ...They have a zeal of God, but not according to knowledge.

    B. What else is needed?

    _____

VI. Purpose of Knowledge

    A What are three purposes given in the Bible for gaining
       knowledge?

      1. _____

      2. _____

      3. _____

Let your light so shine before men, that they may see your
good works, and glorify your Father which is in heaven.

                                Matthew 5:16

Christ Unlimited — P.O. Box 850 — Dewey, AZ 86327   USA

For whom he did foreknow, he also did predestinate to be conformed to the image of his Son, that he might be the first-born among many brethren.

Romans 8:29

He that overcometh shall inherit all things; and I will be his God, and he shall be my son.

Revelation 21:7

B. Another purpose of gaining knowledge, according to the Apostle Paul is in order to be able _____.

And the things that thou hast heard of me among many witnesses, the same commit thou to faithful men, who shall be able to teach others also.

2 Timothy 2:2

VII. How To Prove All Things

A. According to a dictionary, what are the definitions of the word <u>prove</u>?

1. _____

2. _____

B. As Christians, what is our standard of truth?

_____

Christ Unlimited — P.O. Box 850 — Dewey, AZ 86327   USA

The grass withereth, the flower fadeth: but the word of our God shall stand forever.

Isaiah 40:8

C. The whole world operates on some sort of standard; however worldly standards are doomed, according to Matthew 7:24-27. Why is this true?

_____

_____

D. Our standard, the Word of God, has a twofold nature According to John 1:1-4 and 2 Timothy 3:14-17, what are these?

1. _____

2. _____

E. Why must we be totally committed to the Living Word, Jesus Christ, if we are to be able to discern truth from error?

_____

. . . . I am the way, the truth and the life ... .

John 14:6

Christ Unlimited — P.O. Box 850 — Dewey, AZ 86327   USA

F. Who is a true disciple and learner of Jesus?

_____

Then said Jesus to those Jews which believed on him, If ye continue in my word, then are ye my disciples indeed; and ye shall know the truth, and the truth shall make you free.

                                             John 8:31,32

G. Who is our Teacher now that Jesus is no longer on earth?

_____

But the Comforter, which is the Holy Ghost, whom the Father will send in my name, he shall teach you all things, and bring all things to your remembrance, whatsoever I have said unto you.

                                             John 14:26

(Also read John 14:6-25)

H. We know that the written Word of God, the Bible, is God's inspired Word. How do we know it is inspired?

    1. _____

    2. _____

    3. _____

References: 2 Timothy 3:15,17

Christ Unlimited — P.O. Box 850 — Dewey, AZ 86327   USA

All scripture is given by inspiration of God and is profitable for doctrine, for reproof, for correction, for instruction in righteousness.

2 Timothy 3:16

Heaven and earth shall pass away, but my words shall not pass away.

Matthew 24:35

Remember them which have the rule over you, who have spoken unto you the word of God: whose faith follow, considering the end of their conversation. Jesus Christ the same yesterday, and to-day, and for ever.

Hebrews 13:7,8

I. What are two very important guidelines to learn about God?

    1. _____

    2. _____

And thou shalt love the Lord thy God with all thy heart, and with all thy soul, and with all thy mind, and with all thy strength: this is the first commandment.

Mark 12:30

Christ Unlimited — P.O. Box 850 — Dewey, AZ 86327   USA

Study to shew thyself approved unto God, a workman that needeth not to be ashamed, rightly dividing the word of truth.

2 Timothy 2:15

J. What is the central theme of the Bible?

_____

_____

_____

For God so loved the world, that he gave his only begotten Son, that whosoever believeth in him should not perish, but have everlasting life.

John 3:16

But now in Christ Jesus ye who sometimes were far off are made nigh by the blood of Christ.

Ephesians 2:13

And, having made peace through the blood of his cross... And you, that were sometime alienated and enemies in your mind by wicked works, yet now hath he reconciled in the body of his flesh through death, to present you holy and unblameable and unreproveable in his sight.

Colossians 1:20-22

Christ Unlimited — P.O. Box 850 — Dewey, AZ 86327   USA

Overcoming Life Memory Verses

The suggested memory verses for Section One are:

Beloved, believe not every spirit, but try the spirits whether they are of God: because many false prophets are gone out into the world.

1 John 4:1

Prove all things; hold fast that which is good.

1 Thessalonians 5:21

Review Outline for Section One

I. Proper Bible Study Involves Knowledge and Obedience

    A. There are two kinds of knowledge:

        1. Head knowledge (2 Corinthians 4:4)

        2. Heart knowledge (2 Corinthians 4:6)

    B. Obedience and knowledge are needed along with dedication and zeal (Job 36:10-12; Romans 10:2).

    C. Lack of knowledge brings destruction (Hosea 4:6)

II. The Purpose of Knowledge Is:

    A. To show Jesus to the world, thus glorifying the Father (Matthew 5:16)

    B. To be conformed to the image of Jesus (Romans 8:29,30)

    C. To overcome the world (Revelation 21:7)

    D. To teach others of Jesus (2 Timothy 2:2; Mark 16:15-20)

III. We Must Prove All Things Because of:

    A. False Prophets (Matthew 7:15-23)

        1. Cults

        2. Fads or popular teachings by unscrupulous men (Ephesians 4:14)

        3. Deception (2 Timothy 3:1-9,13)

        4. Man-based traditions (Matthew 15:3,6; Colossians 2:8)

    B. False teachers (2 Peter 2:1)

    C. False doctrines against such basics of the faith as:

Christ Unlimited — P.O. Box 850 — Dewey, AZ 86327   USA

1. Jesus having come to earth in the flesh
   (Matthew 1:21, 1 John 4:2,3)

2. The born-again experience as necessary for salvation and eternal life with God (1 Timothy 2:5,6; Romans 10:9,10)

3. The Holy Spirit and His work in the Church today
   (John 14:12-21; 1 Corinthians 12:1-10)

IV. How To Prove All Things (1 John 4:1-8)

A. By Scriptural patterns:

1. Accuracy

   a. Does the teaching agree with the Bible?

   b. Does it agree by a witness in your spirit?

   c. Is the verse taken out of context to prove a point?

2. Consistency

   a. Does the teaching match similar teachings other places in the Word?

   b. Does it agree with the over-all theme of the Bible - the redemption of mankind?

B. By the "fruit" of the minister's actions and behavior
   (Matthew 12:33-35; Galatians 5:22,23)

1. More "fruit" than imperfections

2. Actions that show fruit

3. Words that reflect the fruit of the Spirit

4. Fruit expressed in lifestyles

5. Fruit expressed in leadership styles (James 3:13-18):

C. Testing to see if a spirit is from God (1 John 4:2,3)

1. Do not believe everything that <u>appears</u> spiritual.

2. Tests to determine if something is of God:

   a. Does it glorify Jesus and His Kingdom?

   b. Even if it is a strong word, was it given in love?

   c. What are the motivations of the person teaching this?

3. Quote what the Word says, not what men say.

4. The <u>Word</u> brings life, not the vessels, no matter how faithful.

5. Every doctrine that does not confess that Christ already came in the Person of Jesus is an "anti-christ doctrine."

V. Testing for False Doctrines

A. Does it agree with the Word of God?

B. Does it witness or agree with our spirits?

VI. Judging One's Calling From God

A. God calls us "to be" before He calls us "to do."

   1. Are we willing to be servants (**Mark 9:35; Luke 22:25-27**)?

   2. Are we willing to give up our own thinking and allow our carnal minds to be cleansed (**Jeremiah 17:9,10; Romans 8:29**)?

   3. Are we willing to be used where we are before trying to go to the "ends of the earth" (**Acts 1:8**)?

   4. Are we willing to be faithful to our calling, large or small, wherever we are (**Matthew 25:23**)?

B. Every Christian has the ministry of reconciliation (**2 Corinthians 5:18-20**).

C. There is a preparation time for everyone.

   1. We must learn to find God's timing for everything.

2. Prepare by studying the Word and putting it into practice (2 Timothy 2:15).

3. Practice the Word in:

   a. Patience

   b. Submission

   c. Faithfulness

   d. Prayer

   e. Waiting upon the Lord (Isaiah 40:31)

   f. Discarding worldly thinking and ways (2 Corinthians 6:17)

   g. Developing the measure of faith that is given to us when we become born again (Romans 12:3)

VII. Dealing With Error

A. We are to judge, or discern, error:

   1. "Judge" no man, but "judge" or evaluate the actions, or doctrines being taught (Matthew 7:1-5; John 7:24)

   2. Judgment should be merciful (Matthew 5:7; Matthew 7:2-5).

   3. Don't go by feelings; go by the Bible (2 Timothy 3:16,17).

   4. Before judging, we should be like Jesus: Ready to lay down our "lives" for those people in mercy (Romans 5:10-13).

B. How to judge with a pure heart:

   1. Study the Bible.

   2. Pray for wisdom and intercede for those in error.

   3. Fast and pray for those in error to be shown truth.

   4. Judge from the Holy Spirit, not from feelings, emotions, or man's thinking.

5. Judge our own actions and attitudes also (Matthew 7:1-5; 1 Corinthians 11:31).

VIII. Judging Supernatural Manifestations

A. Satanic counterfeits for God's supernatural acts produce:

1. Continued confusion

2. Strife and contention

3. Urgency, demanding an instant decision or choice, pushing us into action (God gives us time to pray about choices.)

4. Excitement in the sense realm

5. The condoning of evil deeds and ways

6. Despair and hopelessness

7. Exaltation of the things of the world, resulting in envy, covetousness and jealousy

B. God's operations, listed in James 3:13-18 are:

1. Scripturally based (Romans 12:21)

2. Gentle, not harsh, and bring peace

3. Easily understandable out of His love for us (1 Corinthians 13)

4. Centered in scriptural solutions and righteousness

5. Never glorify people, but are impartial

6. Merciful, sincerely for our good, being His will for individuals, churches, the Church, and society in general

C. We are to "test" and "prove" all things (1 Thessalonians 5:21).

IX. Judging According to the Word

A. Jesus did not tell us not to judge, but rather how to judge.

Christ Unlimited — P.O. Box 850 — Dewey, AZ 86327   USA

B. We are to judge:

   1. With love and mercy

   2. According to the Word

   3. With spiritual discernment and the mind of Christ

C. Concerning judging ourselves, we should:

   1. Deal as gently with other people's faults as with our own.

   2. Not judge too harshly, because every saint has been saved by grace through faith

   3. Know that judging ourselves frees us from His judgment

   4. Consider sins of omission (things not done), as well as sins of commission (overt acts of sin)

   5. Guard against receiving condemnation instead of conviction. The devil condemns. God never condemns, but chastises us two ways:

     a. By His Word (John 12:47,48)

     b. Through the Holy Spirit (Jeremiah 2:19).

29

Review Outline Quiz, Section One

1. What two things are necessary for proper Bible Study?

    a. _____

    b. _____

2. What results from a lack of knowledge, according to Hosea 4:6?

    _____

3. What is the primary purpose of gaining knowledge of the Bible?

    _____

4. List two main things we need to prove according to the Bible?

    a. _____

    b. _____

5. How do we "prove all things?"

    a. _____

    b. _____

    c. _____

6. What are two tests for testing doctrines?

    a. _____

    b. _____

7. List three ways a person should approach his calling from God.

    a. _____

    b. _____

    c. _____

8. To discern truth or error, can we go by how we emotionally feel about the teaching?

    _____

9. Why is it necessary to judge all supernatural manifestations?

    _____

10. If we condemn others or ourselves, are we judging properly according to the Word of God?_____ Why?

    _____

    _____

Prove All Things Workbook

Section Two

"The Bible Is Our Standard"

Christ Unlimited — P.O. Box 850 — Dewey, AZ 86327   USA

Prove All Things Workbook
Section Two: "The Bible Is Our Standard"
Expository Introduction

[Author's Note: The material in this section continues to teach how to prove all things. However, it is not taken from one of the books in this course on the overcoming Christian life, but is added material about the Bible itself and how to use it to best advantage. Answers are provided at the end of the workbook and do not have to be the exact wording in many cases.]

The Bible was written by more than 40 human authors inspired by the Holy Spirit over a period of about 14 to 18 centuries.

All of Scripture was inspired by the Holy Spirit, as we saw in the last section (2 Timothy 3:16). The word inspired in Greek is theopneustos, which means God-breathed.

The Apostle Peter wrote that holy men composed the books of the Bible as they were "moved" by the Holy Spirit (2 Peter 1:20,21).

Also the Apostle Paul wrote to his student Timothy that all Scripture was given by inspiration of God.

All scripture is given by inspiration of God, and is profitable for doctrine, for reproof, for correction, for instruction in righteousness: That the man of God may be perfect, throughly furnished unto all good works.

2 Timothy 3:16,17

Inspiration means that men wrote spontaneously using their own minds and experiences while influenced and directed by God. Today, we have quite a few different translations and paraphrases of the Bible, which will be discussed in the next section.

The Bible is divided into two parts: the Old Testament with 39 books and the New Testament with 27 books. It was written in two different time periods. The New Testament was written over a period of about 60 years, following the death and resurrection of Christ. The Old Testament was written from the time of Moses up to about four hundred years before Jesus was born, when the "book" (scroll) of Malachi was written.

The Old Testament was written in the original Hebrew language, with some chapters in Aramaic. The New Testament was written in Greek with some few phrases also from the commonly spoken Judean language of the day, Aramaic, as opposed to the written language of Hebrew.

The word testament is the King James-era English word for covenant, or contract. Therefore, the books of the Bible are divided according to the two blood covenants God has made with mankind. The old covenant was made between Abraham and God (Gen. 15) and covered Abraham's descendants through Isaac and Jacob, and those in the natural race of Israel who would walk in faith. The new covenant was made with Jesus as the sacrifice; and the mediator between both parties, God and man. A mediator is someone like an attorney who works out the clauses to a contract with both parties.

We recommend R.S."Bud" Miller's book, Covenant: God's Guarantee for Victorious Living, for a better understanding of this important teaching.

The new covenant covers members of all races who will accept Jesus as Savior and Lord by faith. The new covenant fulfilled the promise of the old (Hebrews 8:6) and, ratified by the blood of Jesus, extended God's plan for reconciling man to Himself to cover all races, nations, and cultures (Galatians 3:28,29).

Testament or covenant also can mean what we today call a "will," a last will and testament. So in that sense, the new covenant is the spiritual way in which Jesus left (willed) all of the blessings of Abraham (Gal. 3:14) to those who become born again under the new covenant and are also children of Abraham (Galatians 3:7). In addition, He willed to us redemption for our (Adamic) sin nature. This enables us to become "new creatures" (2 Corinthians 5:17) and have eternal life with God, the Father.

God always has dealt with man through relationships. Adam and Eve were in a personal relationship with God before they fell into sin. In every age afterwards down to Abraham, God has had at least one man (such as Noah) who would come into a relationship with Him and through whom He could execute His plan for the redemption of man.

With Abraham, God "cut" a blood covenant to cover Abraham and his descendants until Jesus would come (Genesis 15:8-21). The ten commandments and the other health, civil, and religious statutes that were given to Israel some four hundred years after the Abrahamic covenant spelled out certain principles God laid down for them to live by and which the Israelites were to obey because of the covenant. This became known as "the Law," which actually was the details of how the covenant would work in the nation and in their lives. The first five books of the Bible written by Moses are not only referred to as "the Law" but is also called the "Pentateuch" in Greek and the "Torah" in Hebrew.

The Law was God's Word for that period and the standard by which man lived in order to receive the blessings or curses of the covenant. In any covenant, there are "assets" or good things that go with keeping it. Breaking a covenant or contract, on the other hand, means trouble, which in Bible terms is called receiving curses. However, Paul made it very clear that the Law never took the place of the Promise (the covenant) to Abraham. Jesus was the "promised seed of Abraham" who was to inherit all of the promises, so through Jesus, all those who are born again also inherit these promises of blessings (Galatians 3:29).

People became a part of the old covenant by being a member of the people of Israel through faith and obedience to God, whether they were born into one of the tribes or whether they joined themselves to one of the tribes (Deut.4:6,13,34; Ex.12:19; and Isaiah 56:3-5). Reading the Old Testament books carefully will show that, even then, the attitude of the heart was more important than legalistically keeping the Law and more important even than being born into Israel (1 Samuel 15:22).

Under the New Covenant, the Law or God's standards are "written on our hearts" (Romans 2:15), which means we have the Holy Spirit within us to remind us of right and wrong. Once we are saved, we have the power to overcome sin through the Holy Spirit and can receive the blessings of Abraham under the new covenant (Gal. 3:14). This is called "living under grace."

However, since the time of Adam and Eve, God has dealt with mankind in two ways: love and mercy (grace) or wrath and judgment. <u>Grace</u> is defined as "undeserved favor." Also, it is the ability to keep the law, which is called "divine enablement." Grace gives us power over sin, according to **Romans 6:14**, because we now have the "Covenant Maker" within us.

Grace does <u>not</u> mean being able to break the law and get away with it. Grace does not mean God looks the other way when we sin. It does mean that if we fail and break the law, forgiveness is immediately ours when we repent. The blood of Jesus already covers us. We can still overcome, although we may not yet perfectly be conformed to His image. We have the power or grace to become the sons of God (**John 1:12**).

Criticism of the Bible Has Been Proven Wrong

Some critics of the Bible say it is simply a collection of man's writings. Others believe it is a great "literary masterpiece," but not the "Word of God." Those are the people who do not believe there <u>is</u> a God. Others believe God's Word is <u>in</u> the Bible but that the entire Bible is not God's Word. However, scholars have proven that the Bible <u>is accurate</u> in its depiction of historical events that have been documented elsewhere, so the rest of it should be considered true in spite of the critics. On the other hand, even if none of the Bible had any secular evidence, we still should believe it rather than the world's knowledge, because it is the Word of God and is reliable.

Reliability depends on the accuracy of a document. There are three tests for determining the accuracy of any document. They are:

1. The Bibliographical Test (the accuracy of the copies that are compared, although there is a time span between them and the originals).

2. The Internal Test of Reliability (the author verifies or disqualifies himself by known factual inaccuracies or contradictions).

3. The External Evidence Test of Reliability (the document is authentic in regard to historical and archeological evidence or other writings).

The Bible passes all three of these tests. Research into formerly unknown languages and excavations by noted archeologists have shown over and over that the Bible is true. Westerners exploring the Middle East for the past one hundred and fifty years and Israeli archeologists since the 1950s have proved the Bible is fact, not fiction. There can be no doubt that archeology has confirmed the accuracy of the Old Testament's historical accounts, in spite of the great skepticism expressed toward the Bible by scholars of the "higher criticism" school (which began with German theologians in the 1700s).

For example, critics said no such place as Sela, the rock fortress (the capital of Seir, home of Esau and the Edomites), existed. From shortly after the time of Jesus until the early 1800s, no one except wandering Arab tribes knew where it was. Then Anglo-Swiss explorer Johann L. Burckhardt risked his very life by disguising himself as an Arab in 1812 and was taken into a hidden valley to a huge rock fortress with only one narrow way in or out. Once again, the Bible was shown to be more accurate than secular history. Today, we know this place as Petra.[1]

Another example is the excavation of Shushan, which lies some 200 miles east of Babylon. It was the capital of ancient Elam (Susiana) and, later, the winter capital of the Persian kings. Sushan was the scene of many Biblical events in the time of Daniel, Nehemiah, and Queen Esther and King Ahasuerus. When archeologists uncovered the floor of the throne room, they found a pavement of red and blue and black and white marble, just as had been described in the book of Esther (Esther 1:6).[2]

The Bible is unique in that it has survived over the centuries with very little corruption to the text. Compared to other ancient manuscripts, the Bible is the most accurately preserved text in existence. The discovery of the Dead Sea scrolls in 1948 has shown the world that if all of the books of the Bible are as accurate as Isaiah — the scroll they have pieced together and dated to 100 B.C. — then there have been extremely few changes since at least a hundred years before Christ. What differences exist between modern versions and the ancient manuscript found in a cave above the Dead Sea are minor ones that make no difference to the text itself and have affected no Church doctrines.

Most disputes among church scholars and theologians involve the <u>interpretation</u> of the words in the Bible, not the words themselves. Because the Bible is the inspired Word of God, it has

Christ Unlimited — P.O. Box 850 — Dewey, AZ 86327   USA

been the most persecuted book in history. A French philosopher, Voltaire, even predicted in 1778 that within a hundred years, Christianity and the Bible would be swept away!

In the days of the French Revolution, the 1790s, a comprehensive effort was made to burn all of the copies of the Bible in the country (the Roman Catholic Latin translation) and thousands of Bibles were burned. However, Voltaire died and is only a name in the history books. France has never again been a really great nation, but more copies of the Bible exist today worldwide than ever before.

The Bible is unique, and it has been proven reliable. One thing that proves it is Holy Spirit-inspired is the fact that, in spite of the diverse human authors having lived across almost two millenia, the theme of the Bible is the same. Although the writing styles vary, the unity of all of the books of the Bible taken together are as if <u>one</u> person wrote them. And <u>one</u> person did — the Holy Spirit.

Compared to other ancient manuscripts, the Bible is accepted as being the most accurately preserved text.[3] The Jewish people preserved the Old Testament manuscripts as no other ancient written documents have been preserved. In fact, most of the other writings from Bible times have been found only in the past few hundred years on clay tablets.

About three hundred years before Jesus was born, the Jewish religious leaders authorized the <u>first</u> translation from the original Hebrew scrolls of the Old Testament. According to Jewish tradition, 72 rabbis and scribes made up a committee which translated the Hebrew into Greek, the common language of the Roman Empire, in

70 or 72 days. This translation is called the Septuagint, from the Greek word for "seventy".

About the year A.D. 500, a group of Jewish scribes called "Masoretes" (so named from the word masora, which means "to hand down" authoritative traditions) took upon themselves the task of ensuring the accurate transmission of the Old Testament to future generations. Located at a school near Tiberias, they established strict rules to be followed by all copyists. No word or letter could be written from memory. The scribe had to look attentively at each word and pronounce it before writing it down. Even the words and letters of each section were counted, and if these did not add up to the newly made copy, that section was discarded and copying started over.

The Jewish scribes had the responsibility for copying the old scrolls as they became cracked and not able to be used. Modern scholars have discovered several hundred copying errors, but most of those were made after the time of Jesus by monks who copied the early scrolls and codex manuscripts. The first scrolls were animal skins scraped thin and made into pages that were bound side by side and rolled up. Later, scrolls were papyrus pages. Papyrus was made out of reeds found along the Nile River and pounded to a pulp then dried in the sun. It was the first "paper." Codex manuscripts were sheets of papyrus put together in book form, instead of scrolls.

The majority of scholars agree, however, that the miscopied words do not involve major Bible doctrines. The biggest area of confusion, which involves history, not doctrines, seems to be in the use of numbers. For example, did the Philistines send 3,000 war chariots to one battle or 30,000?

No other book has been so scrutinized, sifted for error, criticized, and even villified and attacked on such a massive scale as the Bible. Yet it is still read and loved by millions.

The Purpose and Theme of the Bible

The Bible's main purpose is to reveal the plan of redemption and salvation for mankind. All Scripture should be studied in this light. Even when the judgment of God is mentioned, it is with the purpose of bringing deliverance to mankind. One of the Bible's purposes is that of warning man, individually or corporately, to avoid the consequences of judgment — God's wrath. If he so chooses, he can escape Hell and go to Heaven.

When studied in the light of God's purpose to redeem man through Christ's death, burial, and resurrection, nothing in the Bible can put us into the bondage of legalism (the keeping of laws in an effort to please God). Law is not the theme of the Bible, but redemption through the grace of God.

People are brought into the bondage of legalism when they stop studying the Word of God with the idea of redemption and salvation in mind. Many people come under bondage, not through reading the Word, but through what someone else has said "the Word says", quoting only a portion of Scripture or quoting a particular interpretation of that verse.

The law reveals our sins, but God's grace points us to Jesus and His blood to cover and atone for our sins, if we will only receive Him and be born again.

Many people want to throw out the Old Testament, except as interesting Bible stories and history; however, the Old and the New work together (1 Cor. 10:11). The Old Testament was not erased; the New was simply built upon it. The redemption plan is told in the Old Testament by "types and shadows." People who were indirect examples of Jesus and the kinds of things He was to do when He came were used as these types and shadows. Also, literal prophecies that directly speak of Jesus fall into this category (Hebrews 10:1).

For example, the temple in the Old Testament was a dwelling place for the Holy Spirit and was a literal building. Under the new covenant, the spirits of those who are born again become God's dwelling place, individually and collectively. Therefore the New Testament speaks of the bodies of Christians as "the temple of God" (1 Cor. 3:16). So the temple that was a building to the Israelites, and later to the Jews, was a shadow, a "picture," of a time to come when man himself could become God's "house" or "temple."

Another example is the word <u>virgin</u> in New Testament typology, which means the holy and pure <u>Bride</u> of Christ (born again believers, or the Body of Christ), who have not had intercourse with the world.

To those who are not Christians, things like this will not make sense. That is why Paul wrote that the natural mind cannot understand spiritual things (1 Corinthians 2:14).

The redemption plan is told in the New Testament through the reports of Jesus' birth, life, ministry, death, and resurrection (Heb. 9:15). Therefore, the Bible's main purpose is to reveal the plan of redemption and salvation for man, which also is the theme of the entire Bible (Luke 24:27,44). The Old Testament was the written preparation for His coming (Isaiah 40:3). The gospels portray the manifestation of His coming (from Jesus' birth to his ascension) (John 1:29). The Acts of the Apostles are the propagation of His purpose or the beginning of the church (Acts 1:8). And the epistles, the letters by several of the apostles to various early churches, presented the knowledge, or explanation, of the mystery of Christ and the hope of glory to Gentiles, those formerly alienated from God.

The Revelation of Jesus to the Apostle John (prophetic visions and words) tells us of the consumation of God's plan, of its successful conclusion in victory, just as Genesis tells us of the beginning being marred by sin. Each part of the Bible needs the others to be complete. Therefore:

The Old Testament was the preparation for the Lord's coming; the gospels were the manifestation of the Lord's coming; Acts was the propagation of the Lord's Gospel; the epistles were the explanation of the Lord's Gospel, and Revelation tells of the consumation of the Lord's Gospel.

Paradise lost in Genesis becomes paradise regained in the Book of Revelation.

Endnotes

[1]Williams, Walter G. <u>Archaeology in Biblical Research</u> (Nashville: Abingdon Press, 1965), p. 55.

[2]Thompson, Frank Charles, Editor. <u>The Thompson Chain-Reference Bible, New International Version</u> (Indianapolis/Grand Rapids: B. B. Kirkbride Bible Co., Inc. and The Zondervan Corporation, 3rd printing, 1984), "Archeological Supplement," #4437, pp. 1692, 1693.

[3]Comfort, Philip Wesley, Editor. <u>The Origin of the Bible</u> (Wheaton: Tyndale House Publishers, Inc., 1992), "Texts and Manuscripts of the Old Testament" by Mark R. Norton, pp. 152,153. Also, Lightfoot, Neil R. <u>How We Got the Bible</u> (Grand Rapids: Baker Book House, 2nd Ed., 1988), pp. 91-93.

Christ Unlimited — P.O. Box 850 — Dewey, AZ 86327   USA

Lesson for Section Two

[Author's Note: All Scripture references that answer these questions have been given. Please do not look at the answer page until you have answered the questions in your own words. This is an expository lesson to help you learn.]

I. Facts About the Bible

    A. From the above expository material on the Bible itself, how many human writers were involved?_____

       1. Who was the <u>real</u> author? _____

       2. Over how many centuries was the Bible written?

          _____

    B. The Bible is divided into _____ sections.

       [Turn to the Table of Contents in the Bible to answer the next three questions.]

       1. How many books are in the Bible?   _____

       2. How many are in the Old Testament? _____

       3. How many are in the New Testament? _____

    C. From the information in the expository introduction, what are the two possible meanings of the word <u>testament</u>?

       1. _____

       2. _____

II. Facts About Covenants

A. What was the Old Covenant?

_____

_____

B. What is the New Covenant?

_____

_____

_____

_____

C. How did people become part of the Old Covenant?

_____

_____

_____

D. How do people become part of the New Covenant?

_____

_____

_____

_____

_____

E. How did the Israelites keep the terms of the Old Covenant?

_____

_____

F. How do we receive the benefits of the New Covenant?

_____

_____

_____

_____

Reference: Galatians 3:13,14

Christ hath redeemed us from the curse of the law, being made a curse for us: for it is written, Cursed is everyone that hangeth on a tree: That the blessing of Abraham might come on the

Gentiles through Jesus Christ; that we might receive the promise of the Spirit through faith.

G. What is <u>grace</u>? (Give two meanings.)

   1. _____

   2. _____

H. How does <u>grace</u> affect the New Covenant?

_____

_____

References: Hebrews 9:14-20; Deuteronomy, chapters 27-30; Galatians 3:13-29; Romans 6.

For sin shall not have dominion over you: for ye are not under the law, but under grace.

Romans 6:14

III. The Purpose and Theme of the Bible

A. What is the main purpose of the Bible?

_____

_____

1. How is the Old Testament redemption story told?

_____

_____

_____

_____

2. How is the New Testament redemption story told?

_____

_____

_____

B. What is the underlying theme of both Old and New Testaments?

_____

Now all these things happened unto them for ensamples: and they are written for our admonition, upon whom the ends of the world are come.

1 Corinthians 10:11

Christ Unlimited — P.O. Box 850 — Dewey, AZ 86327   USA

And for this cause he is the mediator of the new testament, that by means of death, for the redemption of the transgressions that were under the first testament, they which are called might receive the promise of eternal inheritance.

                                        Hebrews 9:15

For the law having a shadow of good things to come, and not the very image of the things, can never with those sacrifices which they offered year by year continually make the comers thereunto perfect.

                                        Hebrews 10:1

Christ Unlimited — P.O. Box 850 — Dewey, AZ 86327   USA

Overcoming Life Memory Verse

The suggested memory verse for this lesson is:

Search the scriptures; for in them ye think ye have eternal life: and they are they which testify of me.

John 5:39

Christ Unlimited — P.O. Box 850 — Dewey, AZ 86327   USA

Review Outline, Section Two

I. The Mechanics of the Bible and Its Accuracy

   A. Divine and human authors

   1. The Holy Spirit inspired the writing (2 Peter 1:20,21).

   a. The Greek word translated <u>inspiration</u> in 2 Timothy 3:16 means "God-breathed."

   b. <u>Inspiration</u> means being influenced and directed by the Holy Spirit.

   2. There were more than 40 human authors.

   3. The Bible was written over a period of 14 to 18 centuries.

   B. Books in the Bible

   1. 27 books in the New Testament

   a. Gospels: the life of Jesus from birth to ascencion

   b. The Acts of the Apostles: the beginning of the Church

   c. Epistles: the writings of the apostles to local churches

   d. Revelation (prophetic visions and words)

   2. 39 books in the Old Testament

   a. The Law or Pentateuch (Greek) or Torah (Hebrew) (the first five books written by Moses)

   b. The Prophets (major and minor)

   c. The Writings: Poetry, history, psalms, etc.

Christ Unlimited — P.O. Box 850 — Dewey, AZ 86327   USA

C. Accuracy of the Bible

　　1. Historically proven by archeological discoveries

　　2. Documentally accurate according to three tests:

　　　　a. Bibliographical (accuracy of copies compared with one another over time)

　　　　b. Internal Test of Reliability (author's facts are accurate and non-contradictory)

　　　　c. External Evidence Test (proved authentic by other historical documents)

　　3. Differences in existing copies of the original manuscripts stem from copyist errors.

　　　　a. Until the 16th century, copies were made by hand.

　　　　b. Errors which are minor do not affect the primary facts or major doctrines of the Bible, but are "typographical" errors.

D. Kinds of criticism of the Bible

　　1. "Higher criticism," a German school of theology from the 18th and 19th centuries that attacked the accuracy of the Bible erroneously.

　　2. Criticism of the entire concept that there is a God, much less a "divinely inspired" written Word of God, which is known as "atheism."

E. Main disputes about the Bible arise from the differences of opinion about it: With varying interpretations of what the words mean.

Christ Unlimited — P.O. Box 850 — Dewey, AZ 86327   USA

1. Mental understanding alone will not prove accurate (1 Corinthians 2:14).

2. Understanding in one's spirit, or revelation knowledge, is the only way the Bible can truly be understood.

3. The God who inspired it, must be the one who gives the understanding of it.

II. The Purpose of the Bible

A. The primary purpose was to reveal God's plan of redemption for man after the Fall:

1. Through two blood covenants

2. His Son's death on the cross to fulfill the old and ratify the new

3. His Son to be the sacrifice, the mediator, and both parties (truly all-God and all-man) to execute the new covenant

4. His Son to defeat the works of the devil (1 John 3:8)

B. The secondary purpose was to reveal in the events and lives of those under the old covenant patterns as examples for the new.

1. The tabernacle and temple as "figures" of believers who are the real temple of God (1 Corinthians 3:16)

2. The lives of heroes and heroines as examples for those born again (2 Peter 2:6; Hebrews 11)

3. The sacrifices and offerings as "pictures, or shadows" of the way the Kingdom of God was to be under the new covenant

4. Examples of how sin and failure brought God's judgment so we would not do the same things they did (1 Corinthians 10:11)

C. Other purposes

1. To give believers knowledge of God's ways and His acts so they can live blessed lives in the earth

2. To give believers knowledge of how God's kingdom is to operate (mainly found in the words of Jesus)

3. To give believers hope for the present and the future with the knowledge of God's ways and our future eternal home in Heaven with God

Review Outline Quiz, Section Two

1. What is the main purpose and theme of the Bible?

   _____

2. Did the more than 40 authors of the Bible write out of their own knowledge, in other words, "head knowledge?"

   _____

3. What does the Greek word translated "inspiration" really mean?

   _____

4. Name one of the three tests by which the accuracy of the Bible has been tested and found to be true.

   _____

5. What is the main cause for differences among believers concerning the Bible?

   _____

6. What was a secondary purpose for God's having the Bible written, according to 1 Corinthians 10:11?

   _____

   _____

7. What is the "temple of God" under the new covenant?

_____

8. What were the sacrifices and offerings of the Old Testament called, according to **Hebrews 8:5**?

_____

9. What does the expression "Bride of Christ" mean to a believer?

_____

10. What is the believer's <u>hope</u> for the future?

_____

Prove All Things Workbook

Section Three

"Bible Translations and Reference Books"

Prove All Things Workbook
Section Three: "Bible Translations and Reference Books"
Expository Introduction

[Author's Note: The material in this section is not taken from one of the books in this course on the overcoming Christian life, but is added material about the Bible itself and how to use it to best advantage, particularly in "proving all things".]

In our lessons so far, we have established that the Bible is our standard as Christians and that it can be trusted and received as the true Word of God. We have no actual handwritten copies of letters or "books" written by Moses, David, Matthew, or Paul, nor of any of the other original authors. Nevertheless, it can be said truthfully that the Hebrew text of the Old Testament and the Greek text of the New Testament are as accurate as men of the highest skill, integrity, and devotion can make them.

In regard to the inspiration of scripture, our doctrinal statement at Christ Unlimited, Inc. is as follows:

We believe that the Holy Bible is the written Word of the living God. We believe it was inspired by the Holy Spirit and recorded by holy men of old. It is infallible in content and a perfect treasure of heavenly instruction which is truth without any mixture of error. The Bible reveals the principles by which God will judge us and His great plan of salvation. It will remain eternally and is the true center of Christian union and the supreme standard by which all human conduct, creeds, and opinions should be tried. Therefore, we believe this Word should go into all the world and should be given first place in every believer's life (2 Timothy 3:16, Hebrews 4:12, 1 Peter 1:23-25 and 2 Peter 1:19-21).

If we truly believe the Bible is the inspired Word of God, then we must go a step further and believe that God has preserved it supernaturally to this day. Frederic Kenyon, a renowned scholar and expert on Bible texts has said:

"The Christian can take the whole Bible in his hand and say without fear or hesitation that he holds in it the true Word of God, handed down without essential loss from generation to generation throughout the centuries." [1]

God knew our need of His Word today, so we must not limit Him to the thought that only the Hebrew and Greek manuscripts are true; but also trust God's keeping ability to preserve a version of those manuscripts for our day. But that presents a problem, as there are many translations or versions available and many portions of those are not in total agreement with one another. So which one can we believe?

My personal preference is the <u>King James Version</u> (<u>KJV</u>), also known as the authorized version, which was translated into English from 1607 to 1611. Before sharing my reasons for preferring this translation, let us look at some other things about the other translations:

1. I believe all translations are used by God; however, not all versions or translations are as pure or as accurate as some others. Personally, I have less problems with the <u>KJV</u>.

Christ Unlimited — P.O. Box 850 — Dewey, AZ 86327   USA

2. None of the translations, including the <u>KJV</u>, are a hundred percent accurate and in perfect agreement with the early Hebrew and Greek manuscripts. However, most scholars agree God has preserved the truths necessary to salvation, the Christian life, and the basic doctrines of the faith in almost every translation.

Six Reasons for Preferring the <u>KJV</u>

In the light of this knowledge of the Word, I would like to share some of the reasons why I read and study from the <u>King James Version</u> (KJV) and why it is my choice and recommendation to all serious Bible students. Following are six of those reasons:

1. The first and most important reason, in my opinion, is that any translation is only as good and as pure as the translators. Many of the other translations had men on their translating boards who were not strictly evangelical Christians or who took their translations from manuscripts whose translators likewise were not doctrinally pure. One example is that many of the new versions have been translated from a Greek version called "the Westcott-Hort Text,"[2] which I consider unreliable because a Unitarian was on the translating staff. I believe his beliefs would have influenced the text.

One so-called "translation" of the Bible is not a translation at all, but a <u>paraphrase</u>. Many people do not realize this when they read The <u>Living Bible</u>. However, Kenneth Taylor, the "author" of this Bible, simply put into his own words what he <u>believed</u> the <u>King James Version</u> says. In other words, it is not a word-for-word

Christ Unlimited — P.O. Box 850 — Dewey, AZ 86327   USA

translation, but a paraphrase, which is "a rewording of the meaning expressed in something spoken or written."[3]

There is nothing wrong with reading a paraphrase, but keep in mind that it is not a literal translation and should not be used for any doctrinal or theological studies. Therefore, I would rule it out for serious Bible students.

Another example of a translation in which I do not have confidence is the Phillips version, The New Testament in Modern English. Although I am sure that the late Dr. J. B. Phillips of England was a devoted Christian and a noted scholar, he did this translation as a young Christian when he did not have the spiritual maturity to attempt such a lofty work.

These are only a few examples, but even from these it becomes apparent that it is very important to have God's approval on the translators, if they are to end up with a divinely approved translation, which brings me to the next point.

2. It would seem to me that God's approval has rested upon the King James Version, because it has had the longest track record of any English version. Earlier English versions are now found only in museums and private collections, not in common usage. The King James, until recently, was the most popular version of all. It has endured all of these years in spite of the attacks upon it. I am firmly convinced that the Holy Spirit played a very definite part in bringing together more than 50 brilliant scholars who produced this translation. These men were the greatest scholars of their day.

To illustrate: John Bois (Boys), one of the translators, was able to read the Bible in Hebrew at the age of five years. He was a proficient Greek scholar at the age of 14, and for years, he spent from 4 a. m. until 8 p. m. in the Cambridge University Library studying manuscripts and languages.[4]

The chairman of the overall committee was Dr. Lancelot Andrewes, Dean of Westminster, who was known as the greatest linguist of his day, being at home in 15 different languages. He spent five hours a day in prayer and was so respected by King James that the monarch ordered all levity to cease whenever Bishop Andrewes was present.[5]

3. The next reason I am sold on the KJV is its global approval. There have been many attempts to replace the authorized version by a translation in more modern English, but as yet, none of these excels the version which has held its place in the English-speaking world for more than 380 years. Therefore, my third point is: the worldwide availability and acceptance of the KJV. At the present time, there are many modern English translations, and yet the KJV Bible is still one of the most popular and most-read versions in the world today.

Some people have objected to the authorized King James Version of 1611 because of archaic words (Elizabethan English) which they felt needed updating. The result was the New King James Version of the Bible. In this version, only words such as "thee" and "thou" were to be changed. However, the translators changed many other words that I believe should not have been touched. So I personally cannot recommend this version wholeheartedly, although it is helpful to students that need assistance in understanding certain usage of words in the KJV.

Christ Unlimited — P.O. Box 850 — Dewey, AZ 86327   USA

However, if we look at the "archaic" words in the New Testament, there are only a few that really need explanation. The Bible tells us in Ephesians 4:11-15 that Jesus gave the Church the five-fold ministry of apostles, prophets, evangelists, teachers, and pastors to teach and minister to the whole Body of believers. It is their job to bring enlightenment and understanding to the various portions of Scripture that need explaining; therefore, the authorized KJV should present no problem to the Body of Christ with God's capable ministers clarifying any archaic meanings or defining the Elizabethan language usage.

One of the most recent books on the various versions and the history of translating the Bible says:[6]

> The Authorized Version gathered to itself the virtues of the long and brilliant line of English Bible translations; it united high scholarship with Christian devotion and piety. It came into being at a time when the English language was vigorous and young, and its scholars had a remarkable mastery of the instrument (talent) which Providence had prepared for them. Their version has justifiably been called "the noblest monument of English prose." (J. H. Skilton, "English Versions of the Bible", New Bible Dictionary, 325-33.)

> Indeed the King James Version has become an enduring monument of English prose because of its gracious style, majestic language, and poetic rhythms. No other book has had such a tremendous influence on English literature, and no other translation has touched the lives of so many English-speaking people for

centuries and centuries, even until the present day.

4. The next reason I recommend the KJV is its ease of memorization. The Elizabethan English into which the Hebrew, Aramaic, and Greek words were translated in this case is an asset, not a detriment. Because of the literary style of that period, the King James Version has a poetic flow that makes memorizing it much easier than other versions.

5. The fifth reason I prefer it is that I believe it has less problems with translation errors than other versions. Although the KJV does have some words and phrases that may be somewhat difficult to understand, it still has less objections to me than other versions, although the Authorized Version certainly requires a dependency on God for understanding some of its verbiage (some of which is made up of mistranslations). Other versions also have the same problem with mistranslations.

In the first century of its printing, many printer's errors were found and corrected in the next printing, but the American Bible Society in the 19th century examined the six editions then circulating of the KJV. The Society found and stated that of 24,000 variants in the text and in the punctuation, none of them "mars the integrity of the text or affects any doctrine or precept of the Bible."[7]

Some people use the supposed mistranslations of the KJV as a reason for preferring newer versions. However, let us look at this "problem" by using an example of such a mistranslation. Perhaps the most well-known mistranslation is found in 1 Corinthians 13, where the word charity is used to translate the Greek word agape. The English rendering of agape is love. This is at once corrected by

God's teachers and scholars who, when teaching, interpret the correct meaning.

Critics say any reader should be able to interpret for himself the correct meaning, if the translation has been done properly. This is true, but the Bible was not written to be read like a common novel. God designed it so that, firstly, we would be dependent on Him to understand His Word, and, secondly, the Body would depend on His five-fold ministry of apostles, prophets, evangelists, pastors, and teachers to help bring understanding (Ephesians 4:11-15).

The Lord desires us to understand His Holy Word, but not to the degree that it is like all other books. His Book must be approached with an attitude of heart that is the key to opening the mental and intellectual understanding of its content. I believe the newer translations definitely have a place to help the new or scripturally uneducated reader. They also help as aids in understanding certain expressions in the KJV that require explanation to be made clear. However, I believe the serious student would benefit more by studying the KJV.

Lest I be chided for being behind the times and appear to refuse progress by sticking with the KJV, I would like to include some computer research information. It seems to verify that, although more modern translations correct some errors, they also create others due to an increase in the vocabulary that is used. I quote from a wonderful computer Bible study aid, the Online Bible Version 4.0:

We have now had enough experience to determine which translation is most suitable to computer word and phrase searching. If one were to rank the <u>NIV</u>, the <u>NKJV</u>, and the <u>AV</u> (or <u>KJV</u>) on this point:

*the AV (KJV) is the best

*the NKJV is good

*the NIV is fair to good.

Much to our surprise, the vocabulary has increased, not decreased, with modern translations and the greater difficulty in finding what you need through a word search. It seems consistency and readability is quite difficult to achieve using modern English. The table below shows the results.

Translation	Words	Vocabulary	Verses
AV, or KJV	790685	12784	31102
NASV	782848	14587	31102
NIV (Br.)	726108	14490	31085
NIV (U.S.)	726109 (?)	14500 (?)	31085
NKJV	770930	13309	31102
RSV	760151	14110	31084

*The RSV deleted 19 verses found in the AV (KJV), but split 3 John 14 into two verses.

In God's omnipotence, He also has made provision for His Word to go out through high-tech communications today and, surprisingly, the so-called "outdated" <u>KJV</u> is the easiest to use for word searches on our modern computers.[8]

6. This brings me to my last point: We believe serious Bible school students need to study and memorize from the <u>same</u>

version when any church or organization is sponsoring a Bible School or course. Standardization is important in maintaining a proper teaching criterion. Students cannot learn in union unless the same standard of measure is used throughout their courses. In our opinion, the <u>KJV</u> meets this standard. Another plus is that it is easy to obtain an inexpensive edition, so everyone can afford it.

Other translations may be used as aids or as additional study material, but only one standard should be used when laying a proper theological foundation.

Having One Standard Is Important for Study

To illustrate, let us look at a sample of several different translations of the following verses:

And they were all filled with the Holy Ghost, and began to speak with other tongues, as the Spirit gave them utterance.

Acts 2:4

For he that speaketh in an unknown tongue speaketh not unto men, but unto God: for no man understandeth him; howbeit in the spirit he speaketh mysteries.

1 Corinthians 14:2

Let us just look at the phrase speak with other tongues in the King James Version of Acts 2:4 and see the different renderings of several different translations:[9]

KJV: Speak with other tongues

MLB: Speak in foreign tongues

TLB: Speak in languages

RSV: Speak in other tongues

AMP: Speak in other (different — foreign) languages.

Now look at the different translations of 1 Corinthians 14:2:

KJV: Unknown tongue

MLB: A tongue

TLB: In tongues

RSV: In a tongue

AMP: (Unknown) tongue.

From these comparisons, without inspiration from the Spirit of God, we can see different theological views could be deduced from the different wording, as there is a big difference between "unknown tongue" and "a tongue" and "foreign languages."

This brings up a subject that should be discussed here. Some teachers try to prove certain doctrinal positions by combing through all the versions looking for one that will prove their point, or view. This is improper handling of Scripture. If a doctrine cannot be proven by the KJV, one should examine the doctrine, not do away with the KJV. Certainly some doctrines can have additional light shed upon them through other translations, but to wrest the scriptures to prove a point is mishandling the Word of God. Some cults have translated and published their own Bibles in order to prove their false doctrines. The Mormons and the Jehovah's Witnesses are two examples of tampering with Scripture.

Some things the new translators have changed are not too significant, while at other times, they have perverted the true Word of God. Let's look at one more example of different renderings in various translations in regard to different meanings that could change what the Bible is saying. The **Song of Solomon 1:3** says:

Because of the savour of thy good ointments thy name is as ointment poured forth, therefore do the virgins love thee.

KJV: The virgins love thee

MLB: Maidens love you

TLB: Young girls love you

RSV: Maidens love you

AMP: Maidens love you

Here again is a vast difference between the words <u>maidens</u>, <u>young girls</u>, and <u>virgins</u>. We know that the Old Testament uses types and shadows to speak about New Testament truths. Doing away with the word <u>virgins</u> totally does away with the type and shadow intended in the Song of Solomon, which is a book that is a type of the Church (made up of virgins) making preparation for her Husband (Christ).

This may seem like a small thing to some; however, when all of the small wordings that are totally different from the <u>KJV</u> are added up, they come to a sizable amount. In many of the new translations, some portions of Scripture found in the <u>KJV</u> are completely left out or they are footnoted with a statement that these words, phrases, or verses were not in some of the earlier manuscripts. (I prefer to trust the manuscripts that the KJV was translated from.)

The New International Version (NIV) is one of the translations that I feel leaves out too much of the Bible as presented in the KJV.

For I testify unto every man that heareth the words of the prophecy of this book, If any man shall add unto these things, God shall add unto him the plagues that are written in this book: And if any man shall take away from the words of the book of this prophecy, God shall take away his part out of the book of life, and out of the holy city, and from the things which are written in this book.

Revelation 22:18,19

What thing soever I command you, observe to do it: thou shalt not add thereto, nor diminish from it.

Deuteronomy 12:32

Every word of God is pure: he is a shield unto them that put their trust in him. Add thou not unto his words, lest he reprove thee, and thou be found a liar.

Proverbs 30:5,6

Christ Unlimited — P.O. Box 850 — Dewey, AZ 86327   USA

I will only give two examples here of important phrases that are missing in the NIV Bible:

And lead us not into temptation, but deliver us from evil: For thine is the kingdom, and the power, and the glory, for ever. Amen.

Matthew 6:13

The NIV does not have:

For thine is the kingdom, and the power, and the glory, for ever. Amen. (It only has the first sentence.)

The NIV totally omits **Acts 8:37**, jumping from verse 36 to verse 38:

And Philip said, If thou believest with all thine heart, thou mayest. And he answered and said, I believe that Jesus Christ is the Son of God.

Acts 8:37

Bible Study Helps

Since we have an enemy, the devil, we can see how he would try to bring confusion in the area of the different versions. We should seek God in this important area as to which Bible versions are better than others. I sometimes use <u>The Amplified Version</u> when I am researching the meaning of certain words, as this translation gives the various shades of meaning possible to different Hebrew and Greek words, and the reader can see these meanings for himself.

There are many good reference works that have been written by men and women under the guidance of the Holy Spirit. Reference works include: <u>interlinear</u> <u>testaments</u> and <u>lexicons</u>, <u>dictionaries</u>, <u>concordances</u>, also Bibles with various study aids.

*<u>Interlinear</u> <u>testaments</u> are those printed in the original Hebrew and Greek with English verbal equivalents printed between the lines. These are good to check exact word meanings.

*<u>Lexicons</u> are dictionaries of the Greek and Hebrew words with all the forms in which they appear in Scripture.

*<u>Bible</u> <u>dictionaries</u> include major words and themes in English with their meanings. However, an <u>expository</u> <u>dictionary</u>, such as Vine's,[10] does not stop with a simple meaning, but gives more definitions, including the various ways the word is used.

*<u>Concordances</u> take every English word in a specific translation and list each place in the Bible where that word appears. They also list the original Hebrew or Greek words and each place where they are used.

The most well-known concordance is the one compiled for the <u>King James Version</u> in the late 1800s by Dr. James Strong of Drew Theological Seminary along with more than a hundred colleagues. This is an almost indispensable study guide for any serious Bible student. Updated versions of <u>Strong's Concordance</u> have become available in recent years.[11]

There also are other concordances available, such as <u>Young's</u> and <u>Cruden's</u>, as well as concordances keyed to the NIV and the NAS.

*<u>Bible helps</u> have been added to many Bibles and contain maps, charts, lists of kings, short concordances, chapter outlines, archeological information, and other helps for more than a century.

The first "helps" added were center columns or footnotes that refer the reader to other places where the word, phrase, or theme occurs. In the last decade, very sophisticated versions of this study aid have been published. There are some new Bibles available in various translations with symbols scattered throughout that mark Messianic prophecies, references to the Holy Spirit, and other major themes.

*<u>Topical Bibles</u>, such as <u>Nave's</u>, are organized by categories of subjects with many of the verses listed or printed out that talk about a particular topic, such as salvation, faith, works, joy, and so forth. These save time for the researcher, who does not have to individually look up the verses in a concordance.

*<u>Additional study aids</u>, are available that will also help in understanding the culture and history of Bible times. There are many books on archeological discoveries, manners and customs in Bible lands, Bible history, and other such subjects.

All of the above study aids allow us to develop several methods of Bible study, such as:

1. <u>Topical Study</u> — which is studying topics such as healing. Looking up the scriptures on this or any other subject, we can see

what God has to say about it throughout His Word, which keeps us from perverting Scripture by taking one isolated verse and building a doctrine on it.

Nave's Topical Bible[12] is an excellent help for this type of study.

Example: Man's choice in relation to being blessed or cursed.

Look up Deuteronomy 30:19,20; Joshua 24:14-21; and Proverbs 1:29-33, as a beginning. These verses will bring an understanding of the importance of choosing God's ways.

2. Typical Study — which is a study of types and shadows in the Word of God.

(A word of caution here, some have taken this kind of study far beyond what it should be and have gotten into error with their fanciful fanaticism.)

To use an example of a typical study: The blood of Jesus runs like a "scarlet thread" throughout the Bible. Looking at a few scriptures such as Exodus 12:12,13; Joshua 2:18,19; Proverbs 31:21; Hebrews 11:26-30; and Revelation 12:9-11. We can see that the scarlet color is symbolic of the blood of Jesus.

The account of Rahab hiding the Israelite spies before the seige of Jericho is an example of the symbology of the blood of Jesus found in the Old Testament (Joshua 2:18-21; 6:21-25). Because she befriended the two men from Israel, she and her family were saved when Jericho fell. The sign she was told to use that would allow the Israelites to know where her house was located was a scarlet thread to be displayed in her window. This was symbolic of the blood of Jesus over her household. Her faith saved her and her family.

3. <u>Character Studies</u> — which is the study of Bible characters whose lives were recorded for our example today. By witnessing their lives, we can see how God responded to their faith and/or their failures and thus be blessed by heeding any warnings, or by following any of their righteous examples.

4. <u>Study of the Books of the Bible</u> — which means understanding the themes, authors, social and cultural backgrounds of the times, and so forth. This is valuable in understanding the full meaning of certain scriptures.

5. <u>Marking and memorizing</u> should also be part of any serious Bible study. Underlining scriptures and making notes in the margin of the Bible is an invaluable aid to remembering specific scriptures and their locations.

6. <u>Study of Names and Numbers in the Old Testament</u> — which is an interesting study for us today, because Hebrew names were not just "labels" but descriptions of people, cities, rivers, and so forth. For instance, the name <u>Judah</u> to a Hebrew means "praise," thus the name itself gives us insight.

Many times the meaning of a name in Scripture leads us to a deeper scriptural meaning when we look it up in a Hebrew dictionary. One small dictionary that is useful for this purpose is

<u>Boyd's Bible Dictionary</u>.[13] Other more exhaustive dictionaries are available in Christian bookstores.

Hebrew numbers also had meanings as they were descriptive and were not like our numbers today which only have numeric value.

The Meaning of Numbers in Scripture

*<u>One</u>: New beginnings and unity.

In the beginning was the Word, and the Word was with God, and the Word was God (John 1:1).

*<u>Two</u>: Witness and division.

<u>Witness</u> — It is also written in your law, that the testimony of two men is true. I am one that bear witness of myself, and the Father that sent me beareth witness of me (John 8:17,18).

<u>Division</u> — Can two walk together, except they be agreed? (Amos 3:3).

*<u>Three</u>: Divinity, Heaven, and God (the Trinity).

For there are three that bear record in heaven, the Father, the Word, and the Holy Ghost: and these three are one (1 John 5:7).

*<u>Four</u> The earth and man.

<u>Earth</u> — And after these things I saw four angels standing on the four corners of the earth, holding the four winds of the earth, that the wind should not blow on the earth, nor on the sea, nor on any tree (Revelation 7:1).

<u>Man</u> — Also out of the midst thereof came the likeness of four living creatures. And this was their appearance; they had the

likeness of a man. And every one had four faces, and every one had four wings (Ezekiel 1:5,6).

*Five: Grace and favor.

Grace — And he took and sent messes unto them from before him: but Benjamin's mess was five times so much as any of theirs. And they drank, and were merry with him (Genesis 43:34). And he commanded the multitude to sit down on the grass, and took the five loaves, and the two fishes, and looking up to heaven, he blessed, and brake, and gave the loaves to his disciples, and the disciples to the multitude (Matthew 14:19).

Favor — And five of you shall chase a hundred, and an hundred of you shall put ten thousand to flight: and your enemies shall fall before you by the sword (Leviticus 26:8).

*Six: The world and man — six falls short of seven; therefore it is imperfection (Genesis 1,2).

Man was created on the sixth day; thus he has the number six impressed upon him. Six also is the number of man's labor apart and distinct from God's rest. It took six days to create the world. 666 is man's number at his zenith (man totaly without God).

*Seven: Spiritual perfection, completeness, fullness, and abundance.

It is used numerous times in the book of Revelation to demonstrate completeness, fullness, and perfection. The mystery of the seven stars which thou sawest in my right hand, and the seven golden candlesticks. The seven stars are the angels of the seven churches: and the seven candlesticks which thou sawest are the seven churches (Revelation 1:20). The letters to the seven churches

(Revelation 2,3) were not only written to literal churches that existed in the Apostle John's day, but also refer spiritually to the Lord's complete Church throughout history. Thus, the messages to those churches are to all of His Church.

*Eight: New beginnings and resurrection power.

There were eight people saved in Noah's Ark to make a new beginning in the earth. Which sometime were disobedient, when once the longsuffering of God waited in the days of Noah, while the ark was a preparing, wherein few, that is, eight souls were saved by water (1 Peter 3:20).

Circumcision was to be performed the eighth day on all new male babies as a token of a new beginning in God's covenant plan. And ye shall circumcise the flesh of your foreskin; and it shall be a token of the covenant betwixt me and you. And he that is eight days old shall be circumcised among you, every man child in your generations, he that is born in the house, or bought with money of any stranger, which is not of thy seed (Genesis 17:11,12).

*Nine: Divine judgment, finality in divine matters.

Man shall be judged on his perfection or lack of it in conforming to the nine fruits of the Spirit. But the fruit of the Spirit is love, joy, peace, longsuffering, gentleness, goodness, faith, meekness, temperance: against such there is no law. And they that are Christ's have crucified the flesh with the affections and lusts (Galatians 5:22-24).

*Ten: Obedience and completeness of order.

Exodus 20 is a record of the Ten Commandments which we are instructed to obey. The tithe, or 10 percent, of a Christian's income represents the whole of what was due from man to God; it marks or recognizes God's claim on the whole (Matthew 23:23).

*Twelve: Government, authority.

Twelve is a product of three (divinity) times four (earthly) which equals Jesus, the King (divine) of kings (on earth). Twelve disciples in the New Testament and twelve tribes in the Old Testament were in authoritative, ruling positions.

*Forty: The number of "testing".

Jesus was tested by Satan after being in the wilderness forty days (Luke 4:2). The Israelites were tested in the wilderness for forty years.

*Three and a half: Spiritually, this is the number of judgment, or the figurative number of an unknown period of perilous times.

In Revelation 13:5, Satan is able to exercise authority for three and a half years, or forty-two months, or 1,260 days, or "a time, times, and an half time" (Daniel 12:7; Rev. 12:14). This period of time can be symbolic. Jewish scribes used three and a half symbolically to mean an unknown period of troublesome time.

*Examples of number combinations and their meanings include:

3 x 4 = 12, the union of the divine (God) and earth (man)

10 x 10 x 10 = 1,000, which means complete obedience. In the millennium (the 1,000-year reign with Christ), there will be on the earth complete obedience to God's will.

12 x 12 = 144, which is symbolic of the overcomers of the book of Revelation, the saints who walk in the fullness of God's power and authority with God's mark in their foreheads.

They have been conformed to the image of God with the mind of Christ in them. They have been tested and tried by God.

666 = "the mark of the Beast".

This number is symbolic of man's being marked with Satan's number. Six is man's number. Tripled, it is significant of man's efforts and works without God; man at his unregenerated ultimate — wicked, completely evil. This number also is associated with money and the spirit of mammon, as those who sell out to Satan sell out to mammon (riches).

> Now the weight of gold that came to Solomon in one year was six hundred threescore and six talents of gold.
>
> 1 Kings 10:14

Wealth came to Solomon, yet he declared it was all vanity of vanities (Eccle. 12:8). 666 symbolizes man at his zenith. Humanism, or the world's systems, have marked Satan's people.

For a more complete study of numbers in the Bible, you can read Numbers in Scripture, by E. W. Bullinger. (See Bibliography.)

How To Use Various Translations

Today, since we have a proliferation of Bible translations and many of them are inaccurate in some areas, we should seek God as to which translations we read and study. However, God can use what is imperfect, and I think the simplified English used in some of the modern translations can be very helpful in gaining an overall familiarity with the Bible and an understanding of its basic verses.

When using some of these translations, it is a good idea to cross check them with various other translations and the KJV to be sure the complete sense of what the Holy Spirit intended is made clear.

Remember, some Bibles such as <u>The Living Bible</u> and <u>The Book</u> (which is Christian Broadcasting Network's version of <u>The Living Bible</u>) are not translations, but paraphrases. These can be used for easy reading or for baby Christians but should not be used for serious Bible study or long-term use.

Again, my personal preference is the <u>King James Version</u>. I have used this Bible all of my life, and even as a child, I had no problem understanding the things I needed to know. I feel the <u>KJV</u> is both more consistent in its language and much more of a faithful translation than any of the contemporary versions.

For instance, here is an example contrasting **Colossians 1:14** in the <u>KJV</u> and in the popular <u>New American Standard Version</u>:

In whom we have redemption, through His blood, even the forgiveness of sins. (KJV)

In whom we have redemption, the forgiveness of sins. (NAS)

You will notice that the <u>NAS</u> left out the phrase through his blood, which to me is a very important omission.

How serious are some of the omissions and variations in some of the contemporary translations? Only God knows in the long run.

I am sure there are people who could even read the original texts in the original languages and still not come to the knowledge of God, as the main ingredient to understanding God's Word is the Holy Spirit, who must bring life to the Scripture.

Also, I am sure there are many sincere seekers of God, who

have — and who will — come to know Jesus Christ through any and all of the new versions.

I am thankful that we do not have to be experts in Greek or Hebrew meanings in order to come to a knowledge of salvation through Jesus Christ, which in the first place is a spiritual knowledge, not an intellectual knowledge. However, my advice to those interested in serious Bible study is to use the contemporary translations for cross reference when you would like to examine an alternative phraseology, but study the KJV.

If you desire to research this further, please see the bibliography for the names of books concerning the new translations.

Canonization of the Bible

One last thing all Bible readers should know is how the canon of the Word was determined. Canon (a standard of measurement) in Church terms simply means "the official list of writings considered by the Jews and by the Church as inspired by God." Since there were other godly writings, the Church fathers had to determine those that were inspired by God as opposed to just morally good writings of the day. The Old Testament was settled by the time Jesus was born, some say in the time of Ezra. The New Testament canon of 27 books was decided over a period of time by the early Church. The four gospels and Paul's 13 epistles were settled as the nucleus by A.D. 130. And the New Testament was established as we now have it by A.D. 367.[14]

Christ Unlimited — P.O. Box 850 — Dewey, AZ 86327   USA

Endnotes

[1]Comfort, Philip Wesley, edit. <u>The Origin of the Bible</u> (Wheaton: Tyndale House Publishers, Inc., 1992), "Texts and Manuscripts of the New Testament," pp. 182,193.

[2]Ibid, p. 190. (Westcott, Brooke and Hort, Fenton. <u>The New Testament in the Original Greek</u>, 1881.)

[3]Guralnik, David B., Ed. in Chief. <u>Webster's New World Dictionary</u> (New York: Simon and Schuster, 1980), p. 1031.

[4]Paine, Gustavus S. <u>The Men Behind the King James Version</u> (Grand Rapids: Baker Book House, 1977, paperback version of <u>The Learned Men</u>, published by Thomas Y. Crowell Company, 1959), p. 64-68.

[5]Ibid, p. 20.

[6]Comfort, <u>The Origin of the Bible</u>, "History of the English Bible," pp. 268,269.

[7]Scrivener, <u>The Authorized Version</u>, pp. 36-38.

[8]<u>The Online Bible</u>, Larry Pierce, Woodside Bible Fellowship, 200 Barnswallow Drive, Elmira, Ontario, Canada N3B 3K2.

Christ Unlimited — P.O. Box 850 — Dewey, AZ 86327   USA

[9]Abbreviations used are:

(KJV) King James Version

(MLB) Modern Language Bible

(TLB) The Living Bible

(NIV) The New International Version

(RSV) Revised Standard Version

(Phillips) The New Testament in Modern English

[10]Vine, W. E. Vine's Expository Dictionary of Old and New Testament Words (Old Tappan: Fleming H. Revell Co., 1981).

[11]Strong, James. The New Strong's Exhaustive Concordance of the Bible (Tennessee: Thomas Nelson Publishers, 1984).

[12]Nave, Orville J., Ed. Nave's Topical Bible (Nashville: Thomas Nelson Publishers, 1979).

[13]Boyd, James P. Boyd's Bible Dictionary (Nashville: Holman Bible Publishers).

[14]Cross, F. L. The Oxford Dictionary of the Christian Church (Oxford; New York: Oxford University Press, 1990), pp. 232,,233.

Lesson for Section Three

[Author's Note: All Scripture references that answer these questions have been given. Please do not look at the answer page until you have answered the questions in your own words. This is an expository lesson to help you learn.]

I. The Bible, Our Standard

    A. List scriptures that tell us the Bible is the inspired Word of God.

        _____

        1. What does <u>canonization</u> of the Bible mean?

        _____

        2. By what time was it fully established?

        _____

    B. Are some translations better than others?

        _____

        1. What are some criteria for choosing one to study?

            a. _____

            b. _____

Christ Unlimited — P.O. Box 850 — Dewey, AZ 86327   USA

C. _____

d. _____

2. How are other translations valuable in Bible study?

_____

3. What is a "paraphrased" version of the Bible?

_____

C. Which translation or version does the author prefer?

_____

Give six reasons for this preference:

1. _____

2. _____

3. _____

4. _____

5. _____

6. _____

II. Other Good References and Study Helps

A. List five different kinds of Bible reference or study books:

1. _____

2. _____

3. _____

4. _____

5. _____

B. What is a concordance? _____

_____

1. Are all concordances "complete?"

_____

2. Name the most well-known one.

_____

III.How To Study the Bible

    A. List five different methods of Bible study:

        1. _____

        2. _____

        3. _____

        4. _____

        5. _____

(**Author's Note:** As part of this lesson, the student should select one of these methods as practice. The memory verses at the end of each section can be the beginning of memorizing Scripture.)

Christ Unlimited — P.O. Box 850 — Dewey, AZ 86327   USA

Overcoming Life Memory Verse

The suggested memory verse for this lesson is:

The grass withereth, the flower fadeth: but the word of our God shall stand for ever.

Isaiah 40:8

Christ Unlimited — P.O. Box 850 — Dewey, AZ 86327   USA

Review Outline for Section Three

I. The Bible Is the Word of God

   A. Human writers range from Moses to the Apostle John.

   1. Moses wrote the first five historical books, called "the Torah" by the Israelites and Jews.

   2. The Apostle Paul wrote letters to early churches that make up 13 books of the New Testament. (Some scholars attribute Hebrews also to Paul, which would make 14 books he authored.)

   3. Other New Testament writers are Matthew; Mark; Luke, who wrote Luke and Acts; Peter with two letters; John, with three letters and Revelation; James, and Jude.

   B. The divine writer was the Holy Spirit.

   C. Writing "under inspiration" of God (2 Timothy 3:16) means that the writers used their own minds and experiences but were influenced and directed by God.

   D. The Bible has two sections: the Old and the New Testaments.

   1. Testament means "covenant."

   2. It also means "last will and testament."

   E. The Bible was written mostly in Hebrew, Greek and Aramaic.

II. The Purpose of the Bible: To Reveal the Plan of Salvation

  A. The theme that runs all through the Bible from Genesis to Revelation is Jesus.

  B. The entire Bible reveals that God always has dealt, and will deal, with mankind through love/mercy and judgment/wrath. To receive His love and mercy, we must come to Him by faith and repentance. Rebellion and unbelief bring judgment and wrath.

    1. This was demonstrated through different ways before and after Christ.

      a. Old Testament:

        (1) God's <u>love</u> resulted in His law being written down on tablets for men to see, and His <u>mercy</u> caused Him to provide temporary sacrifices for sin in the form of animals. His <u>grace</u> brought forgiveness when His people turned to Him in faith and repented.

        (2) <u>Judgment</u> resulted when Israel, Judah, and other nations transgressed beyond the bounds of grace and refused to repent because of their unbelief and rebellion.

      b. New Testament:

        (1) His law is written on the hearts of those who have received Jesus by faith (the Lamb of God sacrificed once and forever). Now we have the Holy Spirit and grace within to help us keep God's laws (Hebrews 8:10).

        (2) Judgment falls on rebellion and unbelief today just as it did in the Old Testament, but mercy and forgiveness

are available when we genuinely repent and look to God in faith.

2. Essentially God's ways of dealing with mankind remain the same throughout history.

III. The Various Translations of the Bible

A. Many translations are available today.

1. Most well-known over the years is the <u>King James Version</u>, commissioned in 1611 by King James I, the first king of the combined nations of England and Scotland.

a. The <u>KJV</u> is the first authorized version in English.

b. Previous translations into English were banned and the translators persecuted, even burned at the stake.

2. Christ Unlimited Ministries Bible School prefers the <u>KJV</u> for several reasons:

a. We believe it is more accurate than the others.

b. It has stood the test of time.

c. The translators can be trusted, not only as scholars, but as very spiritual Christians.

d. The language is easy to listen to and to memorize.

e. Traditionally, this translation is the one most people are familiar with, and it has global approval.

3. Other translations may be helpful as study helps, but the Holy Spirit should direct us in using those.

B. Until the 15th century, only a few copies of the Bible in a very few translations were available.

IV. Ways To Study the Bible

A. The Bible may be studied personally or in groups, according to various methods. These are:

1. A verse by verse in-depth study.

2. A book by book intensive study, such as:

a. Cultural settings discovered through Bible reference books on manners and customs, history, and archaeology.

b. Social contexts, researched the same way.

c. Outlining each book for chronological events or categories of subjects.

3. A study of the main characters in the Bible.

a. Personal characteristics

b. What made them great leaders or caused them to fall

c. How they affected the destiny of their nations

d. Why some are considered types of Jesus

4. A study of the various subjects covered in the Bible.

5. A study of events or things that are "types and shadows" of New Testament spiritual events.

a. The early temple, for example:

(1) Every natural thing about it foreshadowed spiritual truths about the Church.

(2) Today, believers make up the Temple of God.

Christ Unlimited — P.O. Box 850 — Dewey, AZ 86327   USA

b. The power in the blood of Jesus:

(1) The truth about His blood runs through the Bible as a prophetic scarlet thread — from the animals killed by God to cover Adam and Eve to the Crucifixion itself.

(2) After the gospels, the <u>effect</u> of the shed blood is presented as an accomplished fact.

6. A study of the meanings of numbers and symbols.

B. The Bible may also be studied through the use of reference books, such as dictionaries, lexicons, topical Bibles, study Bibles, maps, and others.

Christ Unlimited — P.O. Box 850 — Dewey, AZ 86327   USA

Review Outline Quiz, Section Three

1. Which human author wrote the first book of the Bible and who wrote the last?

    _____ and _____

2. Who is the <u>real</u> author of all of the books in the Bible?

    _____

3. The Apostle Paul's "books" were not written as books, but as

    _____.

4. What is the main purpose of the Bible?

    _____

5. Where is God's law written today in reference to believers?

    _____

6. What is the oldest version of Scripture in the English language that is still in daily use?

_____

7. Give one of the reasons why this version is still preferred by many people. _____

8. List at least one method of studying the Bible.

_____

9. Another meaning for the word <u>testament</u> in the Bible is:

_____

10.Name one of the study helps or books available to Bible students.

_____

Prove All Things Workbook

Section Four

"Principles of Interpretation"

Christ Unlimited — P.O. Box 850 — Dewey, AZ 86327   USA

Prove All Things Workbook
Section Four: "Principles of Interpretation"
Expository Introduction

[Author's Note: The material in this section is taken from one of the books in the Overcoming Life Series, Prove All Things. This Expository also contains added material about the Bible itself and how to use it to best advantage. The answers are provided at the end of the workbook and do not have to be the exact wording in many cases. You simply need to make sure that you have caught the concept or principle from the Word of God.]

Interpretation of the Scripture should be done in the light of certain principles.

We must view parts of the Bible in relation to the whole; or otherwise the Bible will seem to contradict itself in certain places. Since the Bible is the work of one mind — the mind of the Lord — it does not actually contradict itself. When we cannot understand something that seems to be a contradiction, it is because of human limitations or a lack of full knowledge.

The first principle and primary rule of Biblical interpretation is:

We must interpret any scripture by other scriptures.

By referring to other verses about the same subject, we can get a more complete picture of that subject.

A good concordance is a great help in studying the Bible. The most well-known one is Strong's Exhaustive Concordance; however, Young's and Cruden's also are good reference works.

The science of interpretation is called <u>hermeneutics</u> from the Greek word <u>hermenuo</u>, which means "to interpret or explain."

Let us use the incident in **Acts 4:18-20** as an example of how to use scripture to interpret scripture where there seems to be a contradiction:

And they called them, and commanded them not to speak at all nor teach in the name of Jesus. But Peter and John answered and said unto them, Whether it be right in the sight of God to hearken unto you more than unto God, judge ye. For we cannot but speak the things which we have seen and heard.

This scripture describes the day when the council of elders in Jerusalem, which had authority over all religious matters, ordered Peter and John not to speak any more of Jesus or of the things He had done. The apostles knew the Old Testament writings told them to submit to authority. Yet, we find them saying they have to speak about the things they saw and heard to be right in the sight of God!

Looking at **1 Peter 2:13-15**, it also seems to contradict what Peter and John did that day in Jerusalem.

Submit yourselves to every ordinance of man for the Lord's sake: whether it be to the king, as supreme; Or unto governors, as unto them that are sent by him for the punishment of evildoers, and for the praise of them that do well. For so is the will of God, that with well-doing ye may put to silence the ignorance of foolish men.

Christ Unlimited — P.O. Box 850 — Dewey, AZ 86327   USA

However, by studying the rest of Scripture, we see that Peter's instructions in his first epistle do not really contradict his actions as recorded in Acts. We find from the rest of the Bible there are limitations to submission to earthly authority. We will find that we are not to obey earthly authority, civil or religious, if it contradicts God's authority (**Colossians 1:16-18**).

Other scriptures that show us how to know when to obey earthly authority and when not to are found in:

— Words spoken by Jesus and later recorded in **Matthew 22:36-38**, which told them to love the Lord above all things and all people. Along with that were Old Testament admonitions that the apostles knew well, which said that if someone loves God, he will obey Him.

— Peter's words in **Acts 5:29-33**, where it is recorded that he told the authorities that they "ought to obey God rather than men."

— The words of Gamaliel, one of the religious authorities presiding at the hearing, when the apostles continued preaching about Jesus. The wise priest and scholar said the men should be left alone, because <u>if something is of God, it will stand</u> (**Acts 5:38,39**). In other words, if what Peter and John were saying was not of God, it would not last but die away.

(Please read the three passages of scripture mentioned above before continuing with this lesson. In fact, it would be good to find and read all of the Scripture references mentioned in these lessons.)

Other Principles of Interpretation

A <u>second</u> principle of interpretation then is to establish a fact or truth in the mouth of two or three witnesses in referring to Scripture. This means there should be at least two or three scriptures verifying a doctrine or principle (Deuteronomy 17:6, 19:15; Matthew 18:16; 2 Corinthians 13:1; 1 Timothy 5:19; Hebrews 10:28). It takes more than one scripture to prove a doctrine, a point, or a principle.

Another good way to use your concordance is to make a topical study of any subject to see what God's Word has to say in different places on a particular subject or topic. Most Bibles have small concordances in the back of them so you can look up different topics to get a broad view of that subject. However, you need a larger one, such as <u>Strong's</u>, to research a topic thoroughly.

The third important principle of interpretation is known as: "The Law of First Mention." In testing Scripture by Scripture, it is important to look for the place in the Bible that a subject, attitude, or principle is mentioned for the first time and see what it meant there. "The Law of the First Mention" states that wherever a concept or topic is first introduced in Scripture, there are certain foundational principles laid down by that first mention, which govern and fulfill it. It is like a legal case that is settled in the Supreme Court. Once a decision is reached on that case it becomes a "landmark case." "Landmark cases" then set a precedent for future cases. In the study of any topic in scripture we should find where that topic is "first mentioned" and build our study on that foundation. Again, this requires looking up words or phrases in a concordance.

Some other guidelines of interpretation are:

1. Scripture should always be accepted literally unless it is clearly figurative or symbolic. "Spiritualizing" too much can dilute God's Word, while "literalizing" too much can bring bondage and legalism. The Holy Spirit is our guide.

   For example, in **Revelation 12:4**, Satan is described as being cast out of Heaven with a third part of the "stars" going with him. To understand what this means, let us first apply the "Law of First Mention". Going to the concordance, we find the word <u>stars</u> "first mentioned" in the book of Revelation in **Revelation 1:20**. We see in that verse the interpretation for stars is "angels, or messengers of God." We use the first mention in Revelation, instead of the first mention in Genesis, because Revelation is full of <u>symbolic pictures</u> of literal things, while Genesis is a book describing literal events. We now can understand the interpretation that one-third of the <u>stars</u> means "angels," and therefore, they were cast out of Heaven with Lucifer (the dragon) to the earth.

2. We should pray and ask the Holy Spirit to illuminate the Word to us before beginning any study. Then we can understand by revelation. The Lord at times may speak a direct message to us from His Word (which will be the application of His Word to our spirits).

Christ Unlimited — P.O. Box 850 — Dewey, AZ 86327   USA

3. We should not use the Bible for "fortune telling". Some people open the Bible to a page, then point to a verse with their eyes closed, and use that for guidance and direction. Sometimes, for "baby" Christians, God will go ahead and give them a message that way, but continued use of that method amounts to fortune-telling, much like reading tea leaves, and the enemy will get involved sooner or later.

   In seeking God for direction, it is permissable to ask the Lord to lead us to a scripture in the Bible that will help us find the answer to our current problem.

   One of the best way to get answers from God is to spend time daily in prayer and studying the Word; then in those times, the Holy Spirit will lead us to, or remind us of, certain scriptures.

4. Trust God's Word above all else. We must believe fully in the integrity of God's Word and give it first place, if we are to know the God who wrote it. A new Christian will not understand the Word as well as a mature Christian, who has studied the Bible enough to get an understanding in his spirit of the way God thinks and acts.

Here are some scriptures from the Word written by four different men who were inspired of God. Their writings covered a period of time ranging over about 1,500 years, yet each of them verify the faithfulness of God's Word to us.

… Or hath he spoken, and shall he not make it good?

Numbers 23:19 (Moses)

Christ Unlimited — P.O. Box 850 — Dewey, AZ 86327   USA

The words of the Lord are pure words: as silver tried in a furnace of earth, purified seven times. Thou shalt keep them, O Lord, thou shalt preserve them from this generation for ever.... Thou hast magnified thy word above all thy name.

Psalms 12:6,7; 138:2 (David)

...I will hasten my word to perform it.

Jeremiah 1:12 (Jeremiah)

...The scripture cannot be broken. ...Thy word is truth.

John 10:35; 17:17

(the Apostle John)

It takes trust that God wants to open up His Word to you, and faithfulness in studying it and waiting on Him to gain true understanding and knowledge (John 6:51,52,60,66; Hebrews 5:12-14). It does not make any difference what things look like, if God said it, He will do it. Although what we see happening is beyond our personal experiences with God, we should still choose to believe God's Word in spite of our lack of understanding (Proverbs 3:5).

In addition to the Bible itself, we can and should use and appreciate the writings and works of godly men and women throughout history. They were raised up by God to teach others the knowledge of His Word and to lead others in faith (Ephesians 4:11-15; 2 Timothy 2:2).

One example of a Christian work outside the Bible that has lasted for more than two hundred years and has been invaluable to

Christ Unlimited — P.O. Box 850 — Dewey, AZ 86327   USA

many is the classic, <u>Pilgrim's Progress</u>, by John Bunyan. This is a very good book that gives a graphic picture of the overcoming Christian walk through this world.

However, even in listening to men and women of God or in reading their works, we must <u>prove</u> what we hear to be scriptural. That is a Christian's individual responsibility, as we saw in an earlier lesson. Some scriptures that tell us how to do this, in addition to the material in earlier sections, are: Mark 4:24, Matthew 7:20, and Matthew 12:33.

In addition, here are some practical guidelines for "proving" or "testing" those who teach or preach:

1. Notice the words of their mouths. Jesus said that the mouth speaks out of the abundance of the heart (Matthew 12:34).

2. Notice their lifestyles (Matthew 12:33).

3. Notice the fruits of their spirits (Galatians 5:22,23).

On the other hand, do not expect perfection in any leader. No man or woman has all the truth or is to the place where God is not working in them any longer. There was only one perfect man: Jesus Christ. Men will fail at some time or other. Only God, the Holy Spirit, and Jesus will never fail us.

If leaders are put up on pedestals as "stars" or "heroes and heroines," our expectations will sooner or later turn to disillusionment, and then we will be tempted to judge them. However, we may look to them as godly role models and as examples, when we see Jesus demonstrated in their lives.

Here are some more "don'ts" concerning our right attitudes to leaders:

Christ Unlimited — P.O. Box 850 — Dewey, AZ 86327   USA

— Do not exalt spiritual leaders as special persons, but do honor and respect their offices in Jesus and listen to them.

— Do not put them above God.

— Do not expect them to do our praying for us.

— Do not expect them to make decisions for us. Check out any counsel with the Word, and remember that we are individually accountable to God for our personal choices and decisions. They may help us come to right decisions based on the Word of God.

— Do not refuse all of a teaching or all of their advice simply because it is not possible to agree with part of it. We should accept what is right and throw out the rest — if we <u>know</u> it is not right. However, if the part we cannot accept is something we may not yet understand, then we would be wise to lay it aside for the time being and study to understand it.

— Do not have an unteachable spirit so that truth cannot be received when it comes in different teaching or preaching styles or in a different type of word usage.

— Do not accept a teaching if it does not glorify Jesus and His kingdom. However, a hard word that glorifies God and His Word can be God's correction to us, when it is movtivated by love for us. Test the spirit (attitude) of the person delivering that word.

We also need to test or prove our calling from God. If we truly are called of God to do a special work for Him, we must know the answers to the following questions:

1) What has God called me to do?

2) When does He want me to do it?

Christ Unlimited — P.O. Box 850 — Dewey, AZ 86327   USA

3) How does He want me to do it? (In other words, what is <u>His</u> plan for doing this work?)

In conclusion, then, principles for interpreting the Bible are:

1. Let Scripture interpret Scripture.
2. Prove an interpretation in the mouth of two or three witnesses.
3. Find the first time a certain subject is mentioned in Scripture and study that for its fuller meaning (the law of first mention).
4. Take the Bible literally wherever possible and as it makes sense. Consider it from the standpoint of God's power, ability, and character.
5. Gain familiarity with the Bible as a whole. In other words, get to know the "forest," not just what some individual "trees" look like.
6. Do not handle the Word of God deceitfully (2 Corinthians 4:2). We should not try to make it say what we want to hear nor what someone else has told us it says. And, do not use it as "fortune telling."

Lesson for Section Four

[**Author's Note:** All Scripture references that answer these questions have been given. Please do not look at the answer pages until the questions have been answered. This is an expository lesson to help Bible students learn more of the ways and Word of God.]

A. What is the primary rule of Biblical interpretation?

_____

B. Explain the principle to be gained from the examples used in the expository introduction about the Apostles Peter and John and their use of the primary rule of interpretating the Bible.
    (Matthew 22:36-38; Acts 5:29-33, 38, 39)

_____

C. What is the <u>second</u> main rule of Biblical interpretation?

_____

D. What is the <u>third</u> rule of interpretation that directs us to locate or find a topic or concept where it is first introduced in the Bible called?

_____

E. According to this method of interpretation, what would the "stars" of **Revelation 12:4** be referring to?

_____

F. List the other four guidelines given in the expository introduction to this section:

1. _____

2. _____

3. _____

4. _____

G. What is one of God's plans for teaching us His Word, according to **Ephesians 4:11-15** (especially verses 11,12)?

_____

H. In listening to men, what must we first do (**Mark 4:24**)?

_____

I. What is the Biblical test for "proving" men (**Matthew 7:20,12:33-35**)?

_____

J. List the fruit of the Spirit (Galatians 5:22,23).

1. _____   6. _____

2. _____   7. _____

3. _____   8. _____

4. _____   9. _____

5. _____

K. What are some practical guidelines for proving or testing spiritual
    leaders?

1. _____

2. _____

3. _____

L. What is the proper perspective to have of leaders?
    (See the "don'ts" in the expository introduction.)

1. _____

2. _____

3. _____

4. _____

5. _____

6. _____

7. _____

8. _____

[Author's Note: For the rest of the Lesson, refer back to the Review Outline in Section One for Prove All Things, as well as to the book itself.]

M. A guideline for proving true or false doctrines can be found in 1 John 4:1-8. [Anti means "against" or "instead of;" Christ means "the Anointed One." So the "spirit of antichrist" in those verses means someone or something that is against or is being offered as a substitute for Jesus, the true Christ, anointed of God as His only begotten Son — John 3:16.]

False doctrines deny:

1. _____

2. _____

3. _____

4. _____

5. _____

Christ Unlimited — P.O. Box 850 — Dewey, AZ 86327   USA

N. We can know if a doctrine is true, if:

1. _____

2. _____

3. _____

4. _____

5. _____

(When the Spirit of God ministers a strong word, it will have God's authority, stability, and love undergirding it.)

O. All supernatural manifestations, such as dreams, visions, revelations, prophecies, voices, and so forth should be tested or proved by the Word of God. We can know something supernatural is not of God, if it:

1. _____

2. _____

3. _____

4. _____

5. _____

6. _____

Reference: James 3:13-18

   a. God's wisdom and His manifestations produce good

      _____.

   b. List some other things from James 3:13-18 that God's
      wisdom produces:

      1) _____

      2) _____

      3) _____

      4) _____

      5) _____

      6) _____

      7) _____

      8) _____

P. Proving and testing our calling from God is a must. We must
know without a doubt the answers to the following questions

Christ Unlimited — P.O. Box 850 — Dewey, AZ 86327   USA

before stepping out into a <u>fulltime</u> ministry (**Romans 12:7.**) If I believe I am called of God, I must know:

1. _____

2. _____

3. _____

Q. <u>Judging</u> is also part of the testing and proving we are to do as Christians. Jesus didn't tell us <u>not</u> to judge, but rather how to judge (**Matthew 7:1-5**). H<u>ow</u> are we to judge?

1. _____

2. _____

3. _____

4. _____

5. _____

R. Some people erroneously believe Old Testament saints were saved by works and New Testament saints are saved by grace. But the law is the will of God, and grace is His undeserved favor and power to do His will. We do not obey the law to be saved, but because we are saved. The law points out sin. Grace saves from sin. Law and grace both are as valid today as in the Old Testament.

Think not that I am come to destroy the law, or the prophets: I am not come to destroy, but to fulfil.

Matthew 5:17

An example of grace in the Old Testament is found in the story of how God dealt with David after he sinned by committing adultery with Bathsheba and having her husband killed.

And David said unto Nathan, I have sinned against the Lord. And Nathan said unto David, The Lord also hath put away thy sin; thou shalt not die.

2 Samuel 12:13

1. How are saints of all ages saved? _____

_____

_____

   a. Define mercy:

_____

   b. Define grace:

_____

2. How are we to judge ourselves?

_____

3. Judging ourselves involves:

_____

_____

4. Judging ourselves frees Christians from being judged by God.

And if any man hear my words, and believe not, I judge him not: for I came not to judge the world, but to save the world. He that rejecteth me, and receiveth not my words, hath one that judgeth him; the word that I have spoken, the same shall judge him in the last day.

John 12:47,48

Thine own wickedness shall correct thee, and thy backslidings shall reprove thee: know therefore and see that it is an evil thing and bitter, that thou hast forsaken the Lord thy God... .

Jeremiah 2:19

a. The judgment of God on evil works can also be expressed as:

_____

(See page 16 of Prove All Things.)

Christ Unlimited — P.O. Box 850 — Dewey, AZ 86327   USA

b. As Christians, who took our penalty for us?

_____

c. If Jesus took the penalty for us, must we still undergo it?

_____

d. How does God chastise His children who are rebellious?

_____

5. In judging ourselves, we must guard against Satan's false accusations, because a) The Holy Spirit reproves or convicts of sin, while b) Satan condemns and accuses.

a. What is the "conviction of God?"

_____

Reference: John 16:8; 1 Corinthians 10:13

b. What is the condemnation of the devil?

_____

Reference: John 3:18-21

6. In judging ourselves, we must not forget the sins of <u>omission</u> as well as the sins of <u>commission</u>.

Christ Unlimited — P.O. Box 850 — Dewey, AZ 86327   USA

Therefore to him that knoweth to do good, and doeth it not, to him it is sin.

James 4:17

a. Define sins of <u>commission</u>.

_____

b. Define sins of <u>omission</u>.

_____

c. Would prayerlessness be sin for a Christian?

_____

Anything short of a total commitment to God is sin.

Christ Unlimited — P.O. Box 850 — Dewey, AZ 86327   USA

Overcoming Life Memory Verses

The suggested memory verses for this lesson are:

Study to shew thyself approved unto God, a workman that needeth not to be ashamed, rightly dividing the word of truth.

2 Timothy 2:15

All scripture is given by inspiration of God, and is profitable for doctrine, for reproof, for correction, for instruction in righteousness: That the man of God may be perfect, thoroughly furnished unto all good works.

2 Timothy 3:16,17

Review Outline, Section Four

I. Interpreting the Bible

A. The science of Biblical interpretation is called <u>Hermeneutics</u>, which means "to interpret or to explain."

B. There are three primary rules of Biblical interpretation:

1. Interpreting one scripture by others

a. Running references with a good concordance enables the Bible reader to determine the meaning of doctrines.

2. Establishing a truth in "the mouth of two or three witnesses"

3. The Law of First Mention

a. Usually, the correct interpretation is found in the way in which a word, phrase, or expression is used the first time it is mentioned in the Bible.

b. Basic doctrines always involve more than one verse.

C. Three secondary rules of interpretation are:

1. Take the Bible literally wherever possible.

2. Study the Word enough to have an understanding of it as a whole.

3. Do not twist scriptures or take them out of context in order to make them prove a pet doctrine or belief.

D. The key to interpretation is revelation from the Holy Spirit

1. The natural mind cannot understand spiritual things (1 Corinthians 2:14).

Christ Unlimited — P.O. Box 850 — Dewey, AZ 86327   USA

2. Only the Holy Spirit can illuminate His meanings from the Word to our spirits and from there to our minds.

II. How To Get Answers From God

A. A major <u>don't</u> in studying the Bible is do not use it as a "fortune telling" instrument.

    1. Some people try to get answers from God by letting a Bible fall open, then picking a verse as their answer.

    2. Or, they randomly select verses by flipping pages.

B. The best way to get answers from God is to study His Word and to pray.

C. The foundation for getting answers is faith and <u>trust</u> in God.

III. Other Sources of Understanding About the Word

A. Writings of godly men and women throughout history

    1. <u>Pilgrim's Progress</u> by John Bunyon is an example.

    2. Sermons by Charles D. Finney and other great preachers

B. Sound Biblically based preaching and teaching

    1. Such preaching and teaching must be judged by the Word.

    2. It must also witness to our spirits.

IV. Guidelines for Testing Other Sources

A. Prove the words spoken by the Scriptures

B. Take a look at the lifestyles of those teaching or preaching

C. Observe the fruits of their spirits

D. Attitudes toward leaders that are not right include:

Christ Unlimited — P.O. Box 850 — Dewey, AZ 86327   USA

1. Putting them up on pedestals, or making "idols" of them

2. Expecting leaders to do the praying, seeking God, or decision making of the sheep

3. Refusing <u>all</u> of a teaching because some few parts of it are in error

4. Having an unteachable spirit toward receiving anything that does not match previously heard interpretations, rituals, or beliefs that are not Biblical but traditional.

   a. Denominational beliefs or teachings of a particular movement can become considered, taught, and believed as if they <u>were</u> in the Bible.

[Author's Note: The Review Outline at the end of Section 1 also covers some of the material in this section.]

Review Outline Quiz, Section Four

1. What is the science of Biblical interpretation called?

   _____

2. How many primary rules of interpretation are there?

   _____

3. Explain the "law of first mention."

   _____

4. What is the key to real understanding of the Bible?

   _____

5. What is the best way to get answers from God?

   _____

6. Name one way of testing other sources of information according to wisdom in the Word of God.

   _____

7. What is another way of judging those who bring the Word of God to us?

   _____

8. What is the primary way to know if a doctrine is true?

    _____

9. What two characteristics must judging be tempered with?

    _____

10. Name one important thing that false doctrines usually deny.

    _____

Bibliography

Bullinger, E. W. <u>Number in Scripture</u> (Grand Rapids: Kregel Publications, 1967, 1992).

Davis, John J. <u>Biblical Numerology</u> (Grand Rapids: Baker Book House, 1968,1991).

Bunyon, John. <u>Pilgrim's Progress</u> (Available in many editions and from several companies.)

Comfort, Philip Wesley, edit. <u>The Origin of the Bible</u> (Wheaton: Tyndale House Publishers, Inc., 1992).

Fuller, Dr. David Otis. <u>Which Bible</u>?, <u>True or False</u>?

Hillis, Dr. Edward F. <u>The King James Version Defended</u>!

Lewis, Jack P. <u>The English Bible from KJV to NIV</u> (Grand Rapids: Baker Book House, 2nd Ed., 1992).

Lightfoot, Neil R. <u>How We Got the Bible</u> (Grand Rapids: Baker Book House, 2nd Ed., 1988).

Paine, Gustavus S. <u>The Men Behind the King James Version</u> (Grand Rapids: Baker Book House, 1977, paperback version of <u>The</u>

Christ Unlimited — P.O. Box 850 — Dewey, AZ 86327   USA

Learned Men, published by Thomas Y. Crowell Company, 1959).

Ray, J. J. God Wrote Only One Bible.

What You Need to Know About
Christ Unlimited Ministries

Purpose and Vision

> Go ye therefore, and teach all nations, baptizing them in the name of the Father, and of the Son, and of the Holy Ghost: Teaching them to observe all things whatsoever I have commanded you: and, lo, I am with you always, even unto the end of the world. Amen.
>
> Matthew 28:19, 20

CHRIST UNLIMITED is not "another denomination," sect, or just a separate group. It is an arm of the Body of Christ — the Church of Jesus Christ, which has been called to strengthen the Body at large. We also believe we have been called to help establish the Kingdom of God in the earth.

CHRIST UNLIMITED is open to help and work with all Bible-believing Christians regardless of their church or denominational affiliations and committed to helping wherever possible in evangelistic and teaching outreaches.

CHRIST UNLIMITED believes that time is running out and the Gospel has not been preached to every creature. Many nations have not heard the Gospel, and in many places, doors for evangelism are closing. We believe it is time all Christians cooperated with the Lord in breaking down denominational walls for a united front line against the kingdom of darkness and in setting up the Kingdom of the Lord Jesus Christ by the power of the Holy Spirit.

CHRIST UNLIMITED provides such tools as to enable the saints of God to establish the Kingdom of God in the earth. We encourage groups of prayer warriors who will pray, fast, and intercede for the nations. This, we believe, is weapon number one. We teach believers how to overcome through spiritual warfare and through knowing how to use their authority in Christ Jesus through the Word and the power of the Holy Spirit.

Christians need to know how to bring down the forces of darkness in their own lives and in the lives of those to whom they minister. We provide such tools as Bibles, literature, **CHRIST UNLIMITED** books, and downloadable audio and video. We promote the Gospel going forth via any means of communication, including radio and video, the INTERNET, and literature. We promote teaching seminars, Bible schools, and correspondence courses, all aimed at winning souls to Christ and building the Body of Christ into maturity.

Bud and Betty Miller serve the Lord together as founders of the multi-vision ministry outreach, **CHRIST UNLIMITED**. The outreaches of this ministry have stemmed from a tremendous desire to see the Word of God taught in its balanced entirety. The Millers are firm believers in prayer and, through prayer, have seen many released from the bondages of fear, failure, and defeat.

Christ Unlimited — P.O. Box 850 — Dewey, AZ 86327 USA

The Millers have a world-wide vision for spreading the full-gospel message and teaching God's Word. Bud not only preaches and pastors a church, but is director of **CHRIST UNLIMITED PUBLISHING**, an outreach dedicated to publishing God's Word in many languages. His experience, openness to the Holy Spirit, and down-to-earth expression of God's love have blessed many. God has endowed Betty with a rare gift of teaching that makes her a practical and effective "handmaiden of the Lord." Both Bud and Betty have hearts turned toward evangelism and missions, desiring to tell everyone of God's wonderful love. Their anointed teaching comes across with simplicity and in the power of the Holy Spirit.

The outreaches of **CHRIST UNLIMITED** are in obedience to the words of our Lord in **Mark 16:15: Go ye into all the world and preach the gospel to every creature.** This mandate from the Lord presents a challenge to our generation as an estimated 25 percent of the world's population still have not heard the Good News of Jesus Christ.[1]

CHRIST UNLIMITED MINISTRIES also is dedicated to teaching God's Word. Hosea 4:6 says: **My people are destroyed for lack of knowledge.** Many Christians are leading defeated lives simply because they do not know God's Word in its fullest.

CHRIST UNLIMITED MINISTRIES has provided literature for those who desire to know God's Word in a greater way. The main thrust of the teaching and literature is directed at "How to be an overcomer." In the endtimes, we must be prepared to overcome the onslaughts of Satan. Many Christians are suffering needlessly, because they do not know how to overcome sickness, depression, divorce, fear, and financial failure. **CHRIST UNLIMITED MINISTRIES** provides answers for troubled families as well as trains workers for service.

DOCTRINAL STATEMENT

> Jesus answered them, and said, My doctrine is not mine, but his that sent me. If any man will do his will, he shall know of the doctrine, whether it be of God, or whether I speak of myself.
>   John 7:16,17

Inspiration of Scriptures: We believe that the Holy Bible is the written Word of the Living God. We believe it was inspired by the Holy Spirit and recorded by holy men of old. It is infallible in content and a perfect treasure of heavenly instruction which is truth without any mixture of error. The Bible reveals the principles by which God will judge us and reveals His great plan of salvation. It will remain eternally. We believe the Bible is the true center of Christian union and the supreme standard by which all human conduct, creeds, and opinions should be tried. Therefore, we believe this Word should go into all the world and should be given first place in every believer's life (2 Timothy 3:16; Hebrews 4:12; 1 Peter 1:23-25; and 2 Peter 1:19-21).

God: We believe in one God revealed in three persons: the Father, the Son, and the Holy Ghost . . . making up the blessed Trinity (Matthew 3:16,17; 1 John 5:6,7).

Man: We believe that man, in his natural state, is a sinner—lost, undone, without hope, and without God (Romans 3:19-23; Galatians 3:22; Eph. 2:1,2,12).

Salvation: We believe the terms of salvation are repentance toward God for sin and a personal, heartfelt faith in the Lord Jesus Christ. This will result in a new birth. Salvation is possible only through God's grace, not by our works. Works are simply the fruit of salvation (Acts 3:19,20; Romans 4:1-5, 5:1; Ephesians 2:8-10).

Body of Christ: We believe the Body of Christ is made up of all who have been born again regardless of denominational differences. We believe in the spirit of unity, while allowing for variety in individual ministries as to their work, calling, and location as directed by the Holy Spirit (Acts 10:34,35; 1 Corinthians 12:12-31).

Blood Atonement: We believe in the saving power of the blood of Jesus and His imputed righteousness (Acts 4:12; Romans 4:1-9, 5:1-11; Eph. 1:3-14).

Bodily Resurrection: We believe in the bodily resurrection of Jesus Christ (Luke 24:39-43; John 20:24-29).

Ascension: We believe that Christ Jesus ascended to the Father and is presently engaged in building a place for us in Heaven and interceding for the saints (John 14:2,3; Romans 8:34).

Second Coming: We believe in the visible, bodily return of Christ Jesus to this earth, to meet His Church (Bride) and to judge the world (Acts 1:10,11; 1 Thessalonians 4:13-18; 2 Thessalonians 1:7-10; James 5:8; Revelation 1:7).

Ordinances: We believe that the two ordinances of the Body of Christ are water baptism and the Lord's Supper (Matthew 28:19; 1 Corinthians 11:24-26).

Heaven and Hell: We believe Scripture clearly sets forth the doctrines of eternal punishment for the lost and eternal bliss and service for the saved — a literal hell for the unsaved and heaven for the saved (Matthew 25:34,41,46; Luke 16:19-31; John 14:1-3; Revelation 20:11-15).

Holy Spirit: We believe the Holy Spirit to be the third person of the Trinity whose purpose in the redemption of man is to convict of sin, regenerate the repentant believer, guide the believer into all truth, indwell all believers, and give gifts to those He wills that they may minister as Christ would to men. We believe that the manifestations of the Holy Spirit recorded in 1 Corinthians 12:1-11 will operate through present-day Christians who yield to Jesus (Luke 11:13; John 7:37-39, 14:16,17, 16:7-14; Acts 2:1-18).

We believe the baptism in the Holy Spirit, with the evidence of speaking in other tongues as the Spirit gives utterance, is for all believers as promised by John the Baptist (Matthew 3:11), Jesus (Acts 1:4-8), and Peter (Acts 2:38-41). The fulfillment of this promise was witnessed by early disciples of Christ (Acts 2:4,10:44-47,19:1-6) and operates in many present-day disciples of the Lord Jesus Christ.

Divine Healing: We believe God has used doctors, medicines, and other natural means of healing; however, we believe divine healing is provided for believers in the atonement made by Jesus' blood shed on the cross (Isaiah 53:5; 1 Peter 2:24). We believe divine healing may be appropriated by the laying on of hands by the elders (James 5:14-16), by the prayer of an anointed person gifted by the Holy Spirit for healing the sick (1 Corinthians 12:9), or by a direct act of receiving this provision by faith (Mark 11:23,24).

MINISTRY FINANCING

> But seek ye first the kingdom of God, and his righteousness; and all these things shall be added unto you.
>
>   Matthew 6:33

We want to share with readers the instructions the Lord gave us in regard to financing this ministry. As this is the Holy Spirit's work, we are to let Him speak to the hearts of people as to what and how much He wants them to give. Quite simply, we are to share the vision He has given us and trust Him to provide for all that we need. We believe the Lord pays for the things He orders, and if He does not order something, we do not want to engage in it. Pray with us that we will stay close to the Lord, and that, in seeking His righteousness, we will be able to hear His instructions clearly as to what He desires us to do. If we do that, we know we shall never lack of the things needed to do His work.

CHRIST UNLIMITED MINISTRIES, INC. is a tax-exempt, non-profit church, established locally in the area of Dewey, Arizona.

[1]Barrett, David B. Cosmos, Chaos, and Gospel (Birmingham: New Hope Publishers, 1987), p. 75.

FOR ADDITIONAL STUDY

This book is taken from a course of Bible studies called the Overcoming Life Series. The entire series is a virtual "spiritual tool chest," as it covers a multitude of subjects every Christian faces in his walk with God. It also answers questions that many believers have concerning the current move of God. These are dealt with in a balanced approach and in the light of the Scripture. God's people are not to live frustrated, defeated lives, but rather they are to be victorious overcomers! Other books available with their companion workbooks are:

PROVE ALL THINGS - Christ warned that great deception would be one of the signs of the end times. In this book, instruction is given on how to recognize false prophets and teachings. Clear Scriptural guidelines are given on discerning the Spirit of truth versus the spirit of error. The book deals with how to judge without being judgmental.

THE TRUE GOD - This is a teaching on the character of God, explaining why God does certain things, and why it is against His nature to do other things. It differentiates between the things for which God is responsible and the things for which the devil is responsible. Our responsibility as Christians destined to overcome is made clear so that we can live victorious lives.

THE WILL OF GOD - This lesson teaches us not only how to know the will of God in our personal lives, family, ministry and finances, but also brings understanding as to why God allows sin, sickness and suffering in the world. As overcomers, Christians are not to suffer under many of the things we have accepted as normal.

KEYS TO THE KINGDOM - Instruction on how to gain authority in God's Kingdom through prayer is the topic of this book. Many principles and methods of prayer are covered, such as praying in the Spirit, fasting and prayer, travailing prayer, praise, intercession and spiritual warfare.

EXPOSING SATAN'S DEVICES - This book is a powerful expose' of Satan's tricks, tactics and lies. Cult and Occultic methods and groups are listed so Christians can detect their activity. Demon activity is discussed and deliverance and casting out demons is dealt with in detail. Satan's kingdom is uncovered and the Christian is taught to overcome through spiritual discernment and warfare.

HEALING OF THE SPIRIT, SOUL AND BODY -This book teaches how to overcome emotional problems, as well as physical ones, and how to receive divine healing. It also teaches how to renew the carnal mind and walk in the spirit of life, thereby overcoming depression, loneliness and fear.

NEITHER MALE NOR FEMALE -What is the woman's role in the church and home? Who is a woman's spiritual head and covering? Does God call women to the five-fold ministry? What does God's Word say about divorce, celibacy and choosing a marriage partner? These and other woman related topics are Scripturally examined.

EXTREMES OR BALANCE? -Many Christians have hurt the cause of Christ through "out-of-balance" teachings and demonstrations. This book shows how to avoid those areas. It also deals wisely with the excesses and extremes in the body of Christ.

THE PATHWAY INTO THE OVERCOMER'S WALK - This book contains answers to the questions an overcomer faces as he presses toward the prize of the high calling in Christ Jesus. How can we be conformed to the image of Christ? How does the Holy Spirit work with the overcomers in the end times? What are the overcomer's rewards?

Write for catalog with pricing for books & companion workbooks plus cassette tapes. We also have electronic books and a condensed Home Bible School on computer diskettes.

Christ Unlimited — P.O. Box 850 — Dewey, AZ 86327   USA

Christ Unlimited — P.O. Box 850 — Dewey, AZ 86327   USA

Prove All Things Workbook

Answers to Lessons and Quizzes

Answers to Lesson, Section One

I.   Definition of Knowledge
    A. Intellectual information gained by the mind
    B. Revelation given by the Holy Spirit

II. Results of Lack of Knowledge
    A. Destruction
    B. Christians

III. Knowledge and Obedience
    A. Obedience — doing and keeping God's Word
    B. Submitted

IV. Learning Knowledge
    A. 1. Are saved with the proper foundation, which is Jesus, the cornerstone
       2. Those who are striving for maturity
       3. Those who are filled with the Holy Spirit
    B. Precept

V.   Submission and Knowledge
    A. No
    B. The knowledge of God

VI. Purpose of Knowledge
    A. 1. To glorify God
       2. To become like Jesus
       3. To be an overcomer
    B. To teach others and thus fulfill the Great Commission (Mark 16:15-20)

VII. How To Prove All Things
    A. 1. To test by experiment or standard
       2. To establish as true
    B. The Word of God, the Bible
    C. Only those things built on <u>The Rock</u>, Christ Jesus, will stand. Everything else will fail.
    D. 1. The Living Word, Jesus Christ
       2. The written Word, the Bible
    E. Because Jesus <u>is</u> truth
    F. One who continues to obey the truth given him
    G. The Holy Spirit, or the Holy Ghost
    H. 1. Scripture tells us.

     2. God has protected it through the centuries.

     3. Its eternal claims that have been proven and work for every age and culture.

I.   1. Love God with total dedication (the <u>whole</u> heart).

     2. Study and give first place to His written Word.

J.   The story of the redemption of man with the cross of Christ as the focal point.

Christ Unlimited — P.O. Box 850 — Dewey, AZ 86327   USA

Answers to Review Outline Quiz, Section One

1. a. Knowledge
   b. Commitment
2. Destruction
3. To show Jesus to the world, thus glorifying the Father.
4. a. Prophets or ministers
   b. Teachings or doctrines
5. a. Scriptural patterns or by the Word of God
   b. Looking at the fruits of those teaching or preaching
   c. Testing to see if a spirit is from God (1 John 4:2,3)
6. a. The Word of God
   b. The witness from the Holy Spirit in our spirits
7. a. Finding God's timing
   b. Prepare by studying the Word (2 Timothy 2:15)
   c. Practice the Word in obedience
8. No. We cannot use our emotions as standards for judging anything spiritual.
9. Because not all that is supernatural is of God (The devil can and does counterfeit God's manifestations.)
10. No. We are to judge ourselves and others honestly but with love and mercy. Harsh judgment brings condemnation, not conviction.

Answers to Lesson, Section Two

1. Facts About the Bible
    A. More than 40
        1. The Holy Spirit
        2. 14 to 18
    B. Two
        1. Sixty-six
        2. Thirty-nine
        3. Twenty-seven
    C. 1. Covenant
        2. Last Will and Testament

II. Facts About Covenants
    A. A contract or agreement between God and Abraham sealed with the blood of animals (Genesis 15:8-21).
    B. An eternal agreement between man and God, made between Father and Son, sealed with the blood of the Son (Hebrews 9:10-28).
    C. By being a part of Israel through faith and obedience to the covenant, whether they were born into the tribes of Israel or had joined them (Deuteronomy 4:6,13,34; Exodus 12:19; Isaiah 56:3-5).
    D. By being born again.
    E. By obeying the laws handed down through Moses because they had faith in God.
    F. Those born again children of God also are to hear and obey God. However, we have received Jesus in our hearts and have the Holy Spirit, who enables us through His power to keep God's principles and commandments and thereby receive His blessings by faith.
    G. 1. The undeserved favor of God
        2. Divine enablement
    H. Because God, through His grace, sent the Holy Spirit as a divine enablement for us to keep covenant with Him.

III. The Purpose and Theme of the Bible
    A. To reveal the plan of redemption and salvation for man
        1. Through "types and shadows," or examples, as well as through direct prophecies of the Messiah to come, the true sacrificial Lamb
        2. Through Christ's life, death, and resurrection
    B. Jesus and His redemptive purpose to save man

Answers to Review Outline Quiz, Section Two

1. To reveal God's plan of redemption for mankind
2. No. They wrote by inspiration of the Holy Spirit.
3. God-breathed
4. Answer may be any one of the following three tests:
    a. Accuracy of copies compared with one another over time
    b. Internal evidence — the author's facts are accurate and non-contradictory
    c. External evidence — proved authentic by historical documents
5. Varying interpretations of words or differences in opinion
6. To reveal in the events and lives of those under the old covenant; patterns and examples for the new covenant believers
7. The body of a believer
8. Types, pictures, or "shadows" of Jesus, the true Lamb of God
9. The Body of Christ, which is like a "virgin" espoused to her husband.
10. Eternal life with God, the Father, Son, and Holy Spirit with all other believers

Christ Unlimited — P.O. Box 850 — Dewey, AZ 86327   USA

Answers to Lesson, Section Three

I. The Bible, Our Standard
   A. 2 Timothy 3:16, Hebrews 4:12, 1 Peter 1:23-25, and 2 Peter 1:19-21
      1. The list of books accepted by the Church as divinely inspired that, together, make up our Bible
      2. 367 A.D.
   B. Yes. None of the translations are one hundred percent accurate; however, some have more errors than others.
      1 a. Select a translation, not a paraphrase.
         b. Select one that has been proven through the years.
         c. Select one, as part of a group, that is in common usage for better group study.
         d. Select one whose translators can be trusted as spiritual, not just intellectual, Bible scholars.
      2. Other translations can be used as helps; in other words, they can be used to compare certain passages for study purposes.
      3. Paraphrased versions are not true translations at all, but rather a man's version, or wording, of what he thinks the Bible is saying; therefore, it is not to be used for accurate or serious Bible study.
   C. The King James Version
      1. The translators can be trusted, not only as scholars, but as very spiritual Christians.
      2. Because of its origin, commanded by King James of England and Scotland as the first Bible authorized in English, and because of its longevity, it seems to have the approval of God upon it.
      3. It is still one of the most popular and accepted versions, being widely available worldwide and has global approval.
      4. The KJV is the easiest of all versions to memorize because of the poetic flow of its style.
      5. It has less problems with translation errors.
      6. Standardization: For a study group, the KJV is the one most people are familiar with traditionally, which makes it easier for everyone in the group to understand what is taught. And it is easy to obtain in an inexpensive edition, so everyone can afford it.

II. Other Reference Books and Study Helps
   A. 1. Lexicons
      2. Topical Bibles
      3. Study Bibles
      4. Archeological discovery books
      5. Books on numbers and symbols in Scripture.

(Each student may have listed different helps from the expository introduction.)

   B. A complete <u>concordance</u> is an alphabetical list of words in the Bible with all of the references listed where each word is used.

     1. No; there are some short concordances that only list the most important words.

     2. <u>Strong's Exhaustive Concordance</u>

III. How To Study the Bible

   A. 1. Study of the books of the Bible (to make a systematic study of each book through outlines, subjects, historical events, and spiritual meanings)

     2. Character studies of various people in the Bible

     3. A topical study (to make a study of various subjects, such as <u>faith</u>, <u>joy</u>, <u>truth</u>, and so forth)

     4. A typical study (to study what numbers or certain symbols mean. There are several books on these subjects available, the most well-known being by E. W. Bullinger. <u>Numbers in Scripture</u> and <u>Figures of Speech in the Bible</u>, Kregel Publications, Grand Rapids, MI.)

     5. Marking and memorizing (to memorize as many as possible of the most important verses)

Christ Unlimited — P.O. Box 850 — Dewey, AZ 86327   USA

Answers to Review Outline Quiz, Section Three

1. Moses and the Apostle John
2. The Holy Spirit
3. Letters, or epistles, to early churches
4. To reveal God's plan of redemption for mankind
5. In the hearts of those who are born again
6. The <u>King James Version</u>
7. Many people believe it is more accurate or other answers in the expository list are also correct.
8. Studying various subjects, characters, individual books and verses, numbers and symbols, types and shadows. (Any one of these is a correct answer.)
9. Covenant
10. Lexicons, dictionaries, map books, books on archeology and Bible manners and customs, commentaries, and others. (Any one of these or others mentioned in the lesson or quiz is a correct answer.)

Christ Unlimited — P.O. Box 850 — Dewey, AZ 86327   USA

Answers to Lesson, Section Four

A. To interpret Scripture by Scripture

B. We must first submit to God, then to men as directed by the Lord.

C. To prove something by two or three witnesses

D. The "Law of First Mention"

E. Angels

F. 1. Scripture should always be accepted literally unless it clearly is figurative or symbolic.

    2. Pray for the Holy Spirit to illumine the Word before beginning to study.

    3. Avoid using the Bible like fortune telling.

    4. Trust God's Word above all else.

G. To raise up men and women in the five-fold ministry of apostles, prophets, evangelists, pastors, and teachers to lead others in the faith and knowledge of His Word.

H. "Take heed" to what we hear.

I. Try, or check, their fruits to see if they are good or bad.

J. 1) Love, 2) joy, 3) peace, 4) longsuffering, 5) gentleness, 6) goodness, 7) faith, 8) meekness, and 9) temperance.

K. 1. Observe the words of their mouths.

    2. Observe their lifestyles. (Should not be extreme poverty or extreme wealth.)

    3. Observe the fruits of their spirits.

L. Proper perspectives of leaders:

    1. Do not expect total perfection.

    2. Do not exalt ministers, but respect and heed them.

    3. Do not put them above God.

    4. Do not expect them to do our praying for us.

    5. Do not expect them to make our decisions, but heed their godly counsel.

    6. Do not refuse all teaching or counsel simply because we do not agree, or cannot understand, a part of it.

    7. Do not have unteachable spirits, so we cannot really hear what is being said.

    8. Do not accept any doctrine or teaching that does not glorify Jesus and the Kingdom of God.

M. 1. That Jesus was born of a virgin

    2. That Jesus bodily is coming to earth again

    3. The fact of Jesus' humanity while stressing His divinity, or vice versa

    4. That one can literally be "born again" in the spirit and be filled with the Holy Spirit

    5. That the Holy Spirit baptism and His gifts are still in operation today

N. 1. It agrees with God's Word.

    2. It bears witness with, or agrees with, our spirits. However, a person must be totally committed to God and sensitive to hear the Holy Spirit for this

Christ Unlimited — P.O. Box 850 — Dewey, AZ 86327   USA

      one to work.

3. We remain humble and trust God to show us His truth (have a teachable spirit).

4. It glorifies and speaks of Christ and His Kingdom.

5. We check what kind of spirit is behind it, which should be one of love.

O. 1. Brings confusion

    2. Causes fear or strife

    3. Produces hopelessness or despair

    4. Excites the fleshy or carnal senses

    5. Speaks of things of the world

    6. Is urgent or demanding

       a. Fruit

       b. 1) Pureness

           2) Peace

           3) Gentleness

           4) Mercy

           5) Impartiality

           6) Sincerity

           7) Righteousness

           8) Easy acceptance or easily entreated

P. 1. What God has called me to do

    2. When He wants me to do it

    3. How He wants me to do it

Q. 1. Mercifully

    2. According to God's Word.

    3. With the mind of Christ.

    4. With love.

    5. Ourselves first.

R. 1. By God's mercy and grace through faith

       a. Mercy requires no punishment.

       b.Grace is God's undeserved favor and His divine enablement.

    2. We are to judge ourselves according to His Word.

    3. Asking for cleansing and forgiveness and confessing our faults to God and to others.

    4. a. The penalty of sin or broken spiritual laws

       b. Jesus took our penalty for us.

       c. No, if He took it, we do not still receive it.

       d. God chastens His rebellious children by His Word and by the Holy Spirit.

    5. a. The Holy Spirit shows us the way out — repentance that leads to forgiveness from God — and extends pardon to us.

       b. When the devil condemns and accuses us, he never leaves a way out. He accuses and dooms us to failure.

    6. a. Sins we overtly commit

Christ Unlimited — P.O. Box 850 — Dewey, AZ 86327   USA

b. Sins of failure to do the things we know we should do
c. Yes, prayerlessness is a sin for a Christian.

Answers to Review Outline Quiz, Section Four

1. Hermeneutics
2. Three
3. Find the first time the word, phrase, or figure of speech is used in the Bible and see what it means in that place.
4. Holy Spirit illumination of Scripture
5. Faith and trust in Him
6. Anything listed in James 3:13-18
7. Look at their lifestyles to see if they are godly or carnal. Are their lifestyles consistent with their preaching or teaching?
8. The primary way to know if a doctrine is true is if it agrees with the Bible.
9. Mercy and love
10. False doctrines usually deny that Jesus was born of a virgin or the fact of the importance of the blood of Jesus.

www.BibleResources.org
Christ Unlimited Ministries
P.O. Box 850
Dewey, AZ 86327
USA

www.ingramcontent.com/pod-product-compliance
Lightning Source LLC
Chambersburg PA
CBHW081513040426

42447CB00013B/3213